THE DECORATED GOURD

THE DECORATED GOURD

GOURD

Beautiful Projects
&
New Techniques

DYAN MAI PETERSON

LARK BOOKS

A Division of Sterling Publishing Co., Inc.
New York

Editor: **Marcianne Miller**
Art Director: **Kathleen J. Holmes**
Photo Styling: **Chris Bryant**
Cover Design: **Barbara Zaretsky**
Photography: **Evan Bracken**
Assistant Editor: **Veronika Alice Gunter**
Production Assistant: **Hannes Charen and Shannon Yokeley**
Illustrations: **Orrin Lundgren and Olivier Rollin**
Special Photography: **Tim Barnwell**
       David Wuttke

To Gary Otto Peterson,
who from Gourd Day #1
was always there,
and to Mom and Dad,
my daughter Ember
Mai Trimble, and
granddaughters
Delaney Mai and
Madison Mai Trimble.

~

Library of Congress Cataloging-in-Publication Data
Peterson, Dyan Mai.
 The decorated gourd : beautiful projects & new techiques / Dyan Mai Peterson.
  p. cm.
  ISBN 1-57990-511-0
  1. Gourd craft. I. Title.
 TT873.35 .P48 2002
 745.5—dc21   2002020209

10 9 8 7 6 5 4 3 2 1

Published by Lark Books, a division of
Sterling Publishing Co., Inc.
387 Park Avenue South, New York, N.Y. 10016

First Paperback Edition 2003
© 2002, Dyan Mai Peterson

Distributed in Canada by Sterling Publishing,
c/o Canadian Manda Group, One Atlantic Ave., Suite 105, Toronto, Ontario, Canada M6K 3E7

Distributed in the U.K. by:
Guild of Master Craftsman Publications Ltd., Castle Place, 166 High Street Lewes East Sussex, England
BN7 1XU
Tel: (+ 44) 1273 477374 Fax: (+ 44) 1273 478606, Email: pubs@thegmcgroup.com, Web:
www.gmcpublications.com

Distributed in Australia by Capricorn Link (Australia) Pty Ltd., P.O. Box 704, Windsor, NSW 2756 Australia

The written instructions, photographs, designs, patterns, and projects in this volume are intended for the personal use of the reader and may be reproduced for that purpose only. Any other use, especially commercial use, is forbidden under law without written permission of the copyright holder.

Every effort has been made to ensure that all the information in this book is accurate. However, due to differing conditions, tools, and individual skills, the publisher cannot be responsible for any injuries, losses, and other damages that may result from the use of the information in this book.

If you have questions or comments about this book, please contact:
Lark Books
67 Broadway
Asheville, NC 28801
(828) 253-0467

Printed in China

ISBN 1-57990-511-0

Contents

Introduction

I ABSOLUTELY LOVE GOURDS. LOVE THEM, love them, *love* them! I'm a self-taught artist. I started with simple tools and the most basic techniques. As I progressed, I developed my own techniques and personal style, and my hope is that you will, too. I believe that when I'm filled up with creativity, I need to give it away so I'll be filled up again. That's why I love teaching and why I wanted to make this book. Sharing my excitement about gourds and my experience with them is one more way to replenish the well of my own creative spirit. Please take my gift to you and run with it.

Many of my students have done just that. And in turn, they've given me the gift of learning how to explain in words

My first series of gourds, 1995, and my first professional photograph, by Tim Barnwell.

what I usually do intuitively in my art. In *The Decorated Gourd*, you'll learn many of the same techniques and processes we practice in our workshops. There are the basic gourd craft techniques, such as dyeing, pyrography, and carving, as well as new techniques I've never published before. Since I love rim treatments, I've included a variety of them, with simple weaving and basketmaking techniques. There are lots of embellishments, too, sometimes just for the sheer fun of making them. Woven throughout the book are many creative and practical tips I've learned along the way.

I love gourds so much that several years ago I decided to create the name of a profession just for gourd lovers. I called it *gourdology*. You won't find it in any dictionary, alas, so you'll have to follow my definition: Gourdolgy is the study of the structure, function, growth, history, evolution, and distribution of the gourd. In other words, the study of the cucurbitaceous family of plants, which many gourdologists love to transform into gourd art.

Although I've been crafting gourds for more than seven years, the possibilities gourds present to the artist are so endless that I will always be a beginner. Some days, especially when you're starting out, you might question why you set out on this path in the first place. You spend half the morning picking out the perfect gourd for your project, and then your dye runs, you carve a hole right through the gourd, burn yourself on the burning pen, send a bottle of purple leather dye spinning across the room, and accidentally knock your finished project off the table, watching helplessly as it falls to the floor and cracks into pieces. Welcome to gourd art!

You just had a bad gourd day. We all have them. The truth is we've gained valuable knowledge from every mistake we've made, since trial and error is our best teacher. After we pick up another gourd the next day, dreaming how beautiful it will be when we apply what we learned the day before, we realize that all our days are good gourd days.

Warm regourds,
Dyan Mai Peterson

> ***There is an old legend that says***
> ***If you give or receive a gourd…***
> ***with it goes all the best in life…***
> ***health, happiness and other good things.***
>
> —sign in the Marvin Johnson Gourd Museum,
> Fuqua Varina, NC

6

THE ORIGIN OF GOURDS

ALTHOUGH GOURDS DECOMPOSE QUICKLY in moist earth, in dry conditions they can last indefinitely. Archaeological discoveries in such arid places as the pyramids of Egypt and ancient cave sites in the Andes Mountains of Peru provide fascinating proof that human beings have been using gourds for millennia.

Gourds were among our first lightweight containers, allowing us to hold water and precious seeds, nuts, and other foods. When we learned how to make clay pots, it was only natural to imitate in clay the shapes of gourds that we knew so well. Scholars theorize that baskets also grew out of our use of gourds. To carry our gourds, we learned to weave suitable vines as simple straps. In stages we eventually covered the whole gourd with vines. The next logical step was to make a container entirely of weavings, without the gourd, thus basketry was born.

In those early days, we used all the parts of the gourd. We ate the small young gourds (in some areas of the world we still do) and we found the seeds to be nutritious food, high in protein and oil. We made medical use of the root, stem, leaf, flower, and the gourd itself.

We cut gourds into all kinds of useful objects, including bowls, spoons, ladles, and strainers. We made music with gourd rattles, drums, flutes, and string instruments. Gourd masks and gourd figures of humans and animals played an important role in ceremonies and rituals.

This gourd ritual doll was used for protection against bad spirits. Tanzania, Nyamwenzi tribe, late 1800s.

Gourds in their natural state are so beautiful they are art pieces themselves.

Today's potters still imitate gourd shapes. **Steven Forbes-deSoule**, *Gourd Shapes*, 2000, raku with silver glaze. Photo by artist

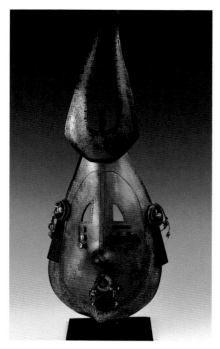

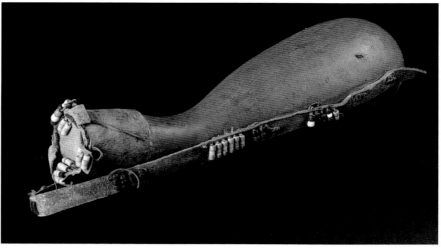

An antique water carrier bottle is lavishly decorated with beads and a hand-made leather stopper.

Dyan Mai Peterson, *Homage to Nature*, 1997, carved, pyrography, gourd beads, found objects, nails, beads.
Photo by Evan Bracken

Art and function in gourds developed hand-in-hand, for decorating the gourd was a natural part of turning it into a useful object. Like other decorated objects, gourds reflected the artistic expressions of the different cultures in which they were grown. In my work, you'll see influences from ancient Africa and Asia, as well as from modern painters.

WHAT ON EARTH IS A GOURD?

A gourd is the fruit of certain members of the cucurbitaceous family, which also includes pumpkins, squash, cucumbers, and all the melons.

Three genera of gourds are the most important in gourd crafting:

1) Hardshell/Lagenaria Siceraria

2) Ornamental/*Cucurbita Pepo*

3) Luffa/*Cylindrica*

Unlike most plants, *hardshell* gourds bloom at night, with lovely white flowers that look like they've been made out of tissue paper. Some of these gourds are known by their shapes, such as the Chinese bottle, banana, short handle dipper, apple, canteen, birdhouse, and basketball gourds. Most of the projects in the book were designed for hardshell gourds.

Ornamental gourds, sometimes referred to as *softshell* gourds, bloom in the daytime, with large orange flowers

Hardshell gourds have white tissue-paper-like blossoms that bloom at night.

that look like delicate trumpets. Their common names include nest egg, crown of thorns, banana, pear, spoon, mini-bottle, and many others. Some of the ornamentals have wildly colorful skins, and are sold in grocery stores as table decorations in the autumn. To preserve their color, these gourds are coated with a clear finish. Sadly, this coating prevents the skin from breathing and soon afterward the gourds will rot. That's why you can't use them in crafts. For craft use, choose unsprayed ornamental gourds straight from your garden or a gourd farm. When dried naturally, the bright colors will fade to lovely tan or off-white shades. In this book I present a few projects made totally with unsprayed ornamental gourds and even more in which I've combined them with hardshell gourds

The *luffa* gourd is a day-bloomer with beautiful orange flowers. When dry, the luffa shell or skin is removed, yielding the sturdy sponge-like interior that makes a perfect washing tool. No wonder it's known many places as the "dishcloth" plant. Luffas are extremely popular as bathing accessories, and I've included a recipe for luffa soap on page 89.

Any support structure can be used for gourds. Light-weight ornamental gourds love my mailbox!

GROWING YOUR OWN ART SUPPLIES

Wherever I teach or demonstrate gourd crafting, whether it be at an arboretum, a gallery, or school, the most frequently asked question is "Do you grow your own gourds?" Like me, the audience is fascinated by the fact that in gourd crafting you can grow your own art materials. We lucky gourd artists can be connected to our art from the very seed of its creation.

I'm a gardener, and most gourd crafters I've met are gardeners, too. Many artists were inspired to learn gourd craft by first coming to know and love gourds in their gardens. Others were gourd crafters first and grew into gourd gardening. Not only are gourds beautiful at every stage of their growth but also, a plus for all us busy folks, they're relatively easy to grow. If you give gourds their basic necessities, all you have to do is, as I tell my students, "Plant and jump back!" Even if you don't grow your own gourds, knowing the process may increase your pleasure in gourd crafting. I could write a whole book about growing gourds (just ask me!). In the meantime, here are some general tips.

The size, color, and thickness of a gourd are determined by several factors: the type of gourd, the genetics of the seed, the soil condition, the amount of water it

Peeled lufffa gourds curing on a clothesline reveal their familiar sponge-like interiors.
Photo by Terry Holdsclaw

You can see the baby gourd just beginning to form underneath the blossom.

The stem has turned brown, so this gourd in my garden is ready to harvest.

After harvest, giant bushel gourds cure on wooden pallets at Harry Hurley's gourd farm. Photo by Harry Hurley

receives, and the weather. United States gourd growers can grow gourds in most of the country's climate zones.

If you've grown squash, pumpkins, or melons (other cucurbitaceous family members) you already know the basics of growing gourds: plenty of sunlight; regular watering; rich, slightly acidic soil; and lots of good, healthy mulch. For more specifics, check with gourd growers in your area and good natural gardening books.

Usually the longer the growing season, the thicker the gourd. Ornamentals, typically much smaller than hardshells, require a short growing season. This means you can often have two crops of ornamentals in the same season.

Once they start growing, gourds need some regular attention. A weeded garden is a good garden for gourds. Strong, healthy vines have a better chance to survive an attack of garden pests, such as cucumber beetles, aphids, cutworms, and vine borers. To avoid using toxic chemicals, just remove insects from the top and undersides of the leaves twice a day.

Thin out weak plants while leaving the strongest. It's the female flowers you want because they produce the baby gourds. If you trim the main vine (which produces the male flowers), you'll promote more lateral vine production, on which the female flowers are produced. To get more blossoms, trim the laterals to promote sub-lateral growth. If you want large gourds with thicker skins, and are willing to have fewer of them, thin the plants out, too. To get even more gourds, be a Gourdparent and hand-pollinate! It's easy and fun. With a soft paintbrush, wipe across the stamen of the male flower and "paint" the stigma (tip of the protruding pistil) of the female blossom.

When the baby gourds form, place a pad of sawdust, paper, or wood under them. This protects them from damage caused to their skin by insects, and impressions made by sticks, stones, and other objects.

No matter how excited you are to harvest your gourds, you'll have to wait until the vine is totally dried because that's when the gourds are completely mature. (If you pick a gourd before it matures, you've stopped its growth and seed production, and it will just rot.) The stems will harden and turn brown, which usually occurs after the first hard frost. Cut the gourd from the vine, leaving a stem about 3 to 4 inches (7.6 to 10.2 cm) on the gourd.

Gourds need to be cured (completely dried) before you can craft them. How long it takes for a gourd to cure depends not only on its drying conditions, but also on its size and wall thickness. Generally it takes several months or more. Large-scale gourd farmers leave their gourds in the field to cure. But if you've grown your own gourds in your garden (like me, you've given names to each one of them and already planned their projects), you want to keep each and every one.

While curing, the gourd skin develops a natural mold. This mold is what gives the gourd its beautiful color and texture. So don't think that your gourd is ruined when it starts getting moldy.

Here's how to tell if your hardshell gourd is totally cured. Pick up your gourd. Shake it. If you hear seeds rattle and the gourd feels light, it's probably ready for crafting.

Some people suggest drilling holes in gourds to speed up their drying. I disagree. The holes invite insects to lay eggs and breed, shortens the time the gourd has to generate its lovely mold, and may cause early deterioration.

Wind, rain, and snow are all elements in the curing process. Photo by Harry Hurley

Gourd Shaping on the Vine

Debra Toth, *Together Forever*, 2000, gourd shaped on the ground, sweet grass, waxed linen, tung oil. Photo by Diane Davis Photography

Long-handled dipper gourd, hand-trained into a knot. Photo by Evan Bracken

Long ago gourd growers discovered gourds would grow into wonderful exotic shapes if they were trained on the vine. Today shaping gourds is an art all to itself. So if you want to create gourd art, but aren't sure if you want to use tools and dye yet, all you need is patience and imagination to train growing gourds into artistic shapes.

The easiest method of shaping is to allow a dipper gourd (usually grown hanging from a trellis to straighten its handle) to grow on the ground; the long handle pushes the ball ahead of it, being forced into strange and wonderful twists and turns as it grows. Some other methods include wrapping the dipper handle around a pole or broomstick to make it spiral, randomly wrapping it with wire (see the Ornamental Gourd Shadow Box project on page 109), or forming it into shapes in square wooden boxes, glass jars, or patterned molds. The possibilities are endless.

Gourds hand-trained with nylon hose, rope and broomstick. Photo by Jim Story

SELECTING YOUR GOURD CANVAS

One reason gourd art is so appealing is that each gourd is unique—each one has its own personality. Gourds interbreed so rapidly when growing that they literally are available in thousands of shapes and sizes and it can be nearly impossible to find two identical gourds—an endless supply of different canvases. The gourd identification chart on the facing page will help you identify many shapes of gourds that are commonly available today.

When I have a design in mind, I start a project by searching for a gourd to fit it. Conversely, when I have a beautiful gourd in hand, I'm inspired to develop a design that will suit the gourd. In either case, what I try to do is help the gourd become what it wants to be.

The lighter in color the skin is, the thinner are the walls of the gourd. The darker the skin, the thicker the walls. Texture varies: some gourds are hard and smooth; others are porous and soft. Handle a few gourds and soon you'll be able to feel the difference in the weight, which will help you to determine the density of the gourd you want for your project.

Gourds are somewhat fragile and can crack or break if dropped. Be careful when carrying a bag of gourds. If they are bumped against each other, they could crack. We call this "bonking." So remember our gourd crafters' caution: No bonking allowed!

When you consider the time, effort, and risk it takes a gourd farmer to produce gourds, and compare their price with painters' canvases, gourds are a great bargain. You can buy gourds at gourd shows, roadside stands, tailgate sales, farmers' markets, gourd farms, through mail order, and on the Internet.

The American Gourd Society Inc. publishes a wonderful educational journal packed with information, crafting ideas, gourd show dates (the most fun events in your entire calendar year), gourd societies (*the* place for gourdologists), and classified ads covering every possible interest in gourds, including an extensive list of gourd farmers who sell gourds and gourd seeds. The farmers are a real asset to gourd crafters. For example, if you wanted a gourd of a specific size and shape for a project, you could merely send a simple drawing of it and they'll be more than happy to find it for you. I haven't met a grouchy gourd farmer yet!

Gourd Identification Chart
1. Hercules Club, **2.** Kettle, **3.** Powder horn, penguin, **4.** Zucca
5. Tobacco box, sugar bowl, **6.** Cannon ball, **7.** Mexican bottle,
8. Basketball, **9.** Canteen, **10.** Wartie, **11.** Lump-in-neck bottle,
12. Apple, **13.** Japanese bottle siphon, **14.** Short handle dipper,
15. Long handle dipper, **16.** Snake, **17.** Chinese bottle, **18.** Maranka,
19. Indonesian bottle, Costa Rican bottle, **20.** Caveman's club,
21. Penis shield, **22.** Luffa, **23.** Bushel basket, **24.** Banana

A typical gourd farm: After you recover from the sight of so many wonderful gourds, you grab plastic bags and start filling them up. Notice the gourd martin houses in the background. Photo by David Wuttke

Dyan Mai Peterson, *Words of Wisdom*, 2000, carved basketball gourd, pyrography, leather dyes, oak handle. Photo by Tim Barnwell

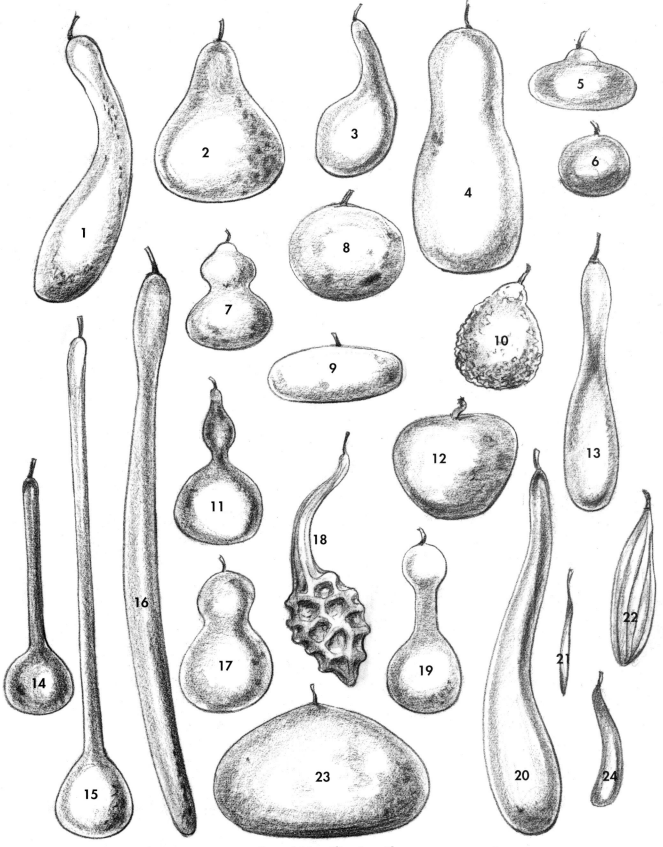

Gourd Identification Chart

Photo 1. You probably already have in your kitchen most of the tools you'll need to clean the outsides of gourds.

PREPARING THE OUTSIDE FOR ART

First you have to start with a properly cured gourd. Then gather the tools you'll need to clean the outside surface of the gourd. See photo 1.

Tools for Cleaning the Outsides of the Gourds

Container to hold water

Scouring pad (stainless steel for hard skins, copper for soft skins

Scraper

Butter knife or dull knife

Scrub sponge

Natural bristle scrub brush

Photo 2. When cleaning the outside of the gourd, be careful not to scratch its surface.

Fill a suitably sized container with plain warm water. Wash tubs, pails, kitchen sinks, laundry tubs, even the bathtub may be used for this purpose. Place the gourds in the water. They float, so cover the exposed surface with a wet towel. No need to add bleach; it smells bad and serves no good purpose. Rotate each gourd in the water every so often to allow the entire surface to soak equally. It may take as little as 10 minutes or possibly several hours for the more stubborn gourds to be ready to clean.

Test the surface with a scrubber. If the dirt and mold come right off, it's ready to scrub. Cleaning the shell of a gourd can be messy, and it does take time, but it's pretty easy, and it's a great excuse to be by yourself and listen to pleasant music. Scrub with a stainless steel scouring pad (or a copper one if the gourd skin is soft) until the dirt, mold, and waxy covering are removed. (See photo 2.) Be careful so you don't scratch the surface. Any concave areas will need special attention. Carefully scrape these places with a dull knife or butter knife. Warty gourds (i.e. maranka or crown of thorns) may require a natural bristle scrub brush. Don't use sandpaper or similar abrasives—they'll scratch the surface. (Notice how smooth the surfaces are in the three red bowls to the left.) If you want to use the stem in your project, carefully wash it and the area where it connects with the gourd body.

Dyan Mai Peterson, *Three Red Bowls*, 1997, carved, pyrography, leather dyes.
Photo by Tim Barnwell

When you're satisfied the gourd is clean, rinse it thoroughly with clean water and set it aside to dry. Drying time varies, anywhere from a few hours to a day, depending on how long you had to soak it. I recommend you wash several gourds at a time so you always have one ready to craft.

CUTTING TECHNIQUES

The proper tools make it safer, easier, and quicker to cut gourds. Here's a basic list of the tools you'll need to cut gourds for the projects in the book. (See photo 3.)

Tools for Cutting Gourds

Gourd-cutting handsaw (see instructions below) made from:
    Saw handle that holds standard reciprocating blades
    18 tpi (teeth per inch) straight (not wavy) hacksaw blade

Small precision jigsaw with a variety of blade choices

Hacksaw

Files, flat or half round, for filing the inside of the neck

Sandpaper, in 100, 150, and 200 grit

Utility knife

Safety glasses

Dust mask

Slip-resistant pad (to hold your work steady)

Photo 3. Proper cutting and drilling tools are essential to safe and efficient gourd crafting. The special handsaw I recommend you make from combined parts is the one with the yellow handle.

In all my years of gourd crafting, I've never found a readymade cutting hand tool that was as safe and effective as I wanted. So I made up my own. Here's how to make one for yourself: Just buy a saw handle that holds a standard reciprocating blade. Then buy a hacksaw blade that is straight (not wavy) with 18 teeth. Insert this blade into the saw handle. Voila! Your own custom-designed inexpensive handsaw. If you are just starting gourdcraft and not sure yet how much money you want to invest in tools, this tool will be just fine. I've listed this tool in almost all the instructions simply as "handsaw."

Once I started making gourds full-time, I realized I needed a more powerful cutting tool. Absolutely essential to me today is a small precision power jigsaw with a variety of blades. You can find it at specialty hobby stores and the Internet. All the other tools you need are probably already in your workshop.

Always wear safety glasses. Use a dust mask when cutting gourds to reduce the volume of gourd dust you might breathe in. To keep your gourd secure while you work on it, lay a slip-resistant pad on your working surface.

The projects in the book use only four styles of openings: 1) Hills-and-Valleys, 2) Bowl-Cut, 3) Straight- or Angle-Cut, and 4) Lidded-Top. In the instructions for each project, I tell you which style of cutting technique to use.

Determine the front (face) side of your gourd. Mark the front with an "X" in pencil for reference. Next decide on the style and size of the opening. Use a pencil for all layout lines. (Mistakes can be erased.)

Design Tips

Always keep the gourd's shape and size, as well as the design, in mind while laying out any opening. Your main goal is to achieve proportion.

Debra Toth, *Romantic Clips*, 2001, carved gourd, leather dyes, gold leafing. Photo by Diane Davis

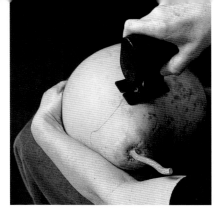

Photo 4. The Hills-and-Valleys cutting technique, accomplished with a precision jigsaw, results in a beautiful and unique rim treatment.

Dyan Mai Peterson, *Evening Flowers*, 1997 (Hills-and-Valleys technique), pyrography, leather dyes, sculptured pine needle rim. Photo by Tim Barnwell

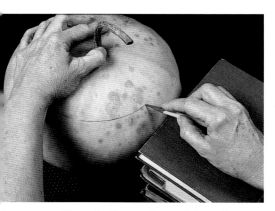

Photo 5. The simple Bowl-Cut technique is standard for functional bowls. To draw an even lid line, create a support that is both steady and easily adapted for use with any size gourd. A column of books is perfect.

Hills-and-Valleys Technique

For the most aesthetic look in this technique, draw an unequal number of hills and valleys. Make the three hill lines around the circumference. Next, draw lines to connect the valley lines with the hill lines, creating a graceful flowing effect. Sometimes it takes a few tries to achieve this. I find it best to be seated while cutting. Support the gourd in your lap and rotate the gourd with the support hand while holding the saw with the other hand.

Drill a starting hole for your blade about 1/4 inch (6.35 mm) away from the cut line, in the waste side. Insert the saw blade into the hole and cut along the line all the way around the top. Try to keep the blade square to the gourd surface. (See photo 4.) There's no need to worry if you don't cut perfectly: the pine needle rim you'll add will cover up any mistakes. When cutting, always extend your blade all the way through the wall into the cavity of the gourd itself to prevent the blade from slipping out.

Bowl-Cut Technique

To cut the gourd into a bowl, begin by studying the profile of the gourd. Usually you'll locate the rim above the widest part of the gourd, where it begins to narrow a bit, at a place that looks the most appealing. This approach yields a strong bowl, yet limits the view into the plain interior. It only takes trying it once to know that you really can't just pick up a gourd and draw a nice even rim line by hand (unless a rugged primitive style is what you want).

Laying out a level line for the rim is easy. Just place the gourd on a flat surface and make a support for your drawing arm so you can place your wrist on it and hold your pencil at the exact spot you want. You can use anything for the support, such as wooden blocks or bricks. I prefer books because I can easily change the levels. Add the support pieces until your pencil, laid flat on the top piece, is even with the desired level of your cut line. (See photo 5.)

Dyan Mai Peterson, *Transformed*, 1998 (Bowl-Cut technique), carved, pyrography, leather dyes, pine needle rim treatment. Photo by Evan Bracken

To create the rim line, hold the pencil firmly and rotate the gourd against the pencil all the way around the gourd. Follow the cutting instructions as described in the Hills-and-Valleys technique above to drill a starter hole, insert your blade and cut along the line. If you are using a handsaw, be careful not to push with too much force or the gourd may crack or break. Sand the rim smooth after cutting. It's a good idea to ease the inside and outside edges of the rim with 150-grit sandpaper.

Angle- or Straight-Cut Technique

Angle or straight cuts are made near the top and through the neck of a gourd. You want the cut line to be in proportion to the size and shape of the gourd and in relation to the design, so first stand the gourd up on a level surface and pencil draw your design on the front. Then pencil draw the cut line all around the gourd, either straight, or at the angle that looks best.

Lay the gourd on its side, supported on a firm surface, such as a block of wood on a non-slip rubber mat. With the hacksaw, make a few short pull strokes to start the cut line, then cut evenly straight through the neck of the gourd. (See photo 6.) Hold the gourd firmly with your free hand while cutting. When finishing the cut, be careful not to chip the gourd's outer surface. File or sand smooth any rough spots.

Lidded-Top Technique

Some projects will require creating a lidded top. I suggested the Hills-and-Valleys cut for the lids in the projects in the book, but you can make your lid any shape you want. The most important thing to remember when cutting a lid is that you'll be cutting the body and the lid at the same time. There won't be a waste side, as in the other cutting techniques, because you'll be keeping the top of the gourd as a lid. Lids may be cut from a vertical or horizontal section of a gourd. If vertical, keep the blade at 90° to the surface.

Use a pencil to lay out the lid rim, in proportion to the size, shape, and design of your gourd. Once you are satisfied with your layout, select a section of the line that is somewhat straight, preferably at the back side of the gourd. Use a sturdy utility knife to carefully score along the line several times, about 1 to 1½ inches (2.5 to 3.8 cm) in length. (See photo 7.) Then carefully rock the blade back and forth into the scored line until the blade pierces through the gourd's wall. This will be the starting point for the saw blade.

You need a thin, narrow, fine-tooth blade for cutting lids, so use either the precision jigsaw or the handsaw with the 18-tooth blade. If you're new to cutting lids, it's probably best to practice on a scrap gourd before attempting the finished piece.

Pierce the blade through the starting point you made with the utility knife and follow the line around the gourd, cutting deliberately. If you stray a bit off the line, don't try to make a quick adjustment. Gradually steer the saw back on the line as you cut. You should do little, if any, sanding because the lid needs to match the body of the gourd as closely as possible.

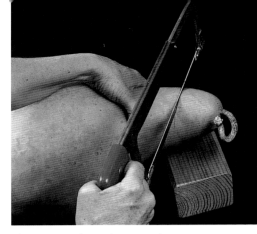

Photo 6. To make angle or straight cuts near the top or neck of the gourd, use a hacksaw.

Dyan Mai Peterson, *Beetles*, 2001 (Angle-cut technique), pyrography, carved, leather dyes, beaded rim treatment. Photo by Evan Bracken

Dyan Mai Peterson, *Lidded Container No. 1069*, 2000 (Lidded-Top technique), pyrography, leather dyes. Photo by Tim Barnwell

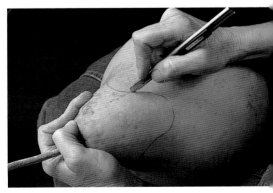

Photo 7. With the Lidded-Top cutting technique, first use a utility knife to make precise starting cuts on the outline of the lid.

Photo 8. Because there are many sizes of gourd openings, you may need a variety of tools to clean the insides of gourds.

The Huichol Indians of Mexico created the lovely interior of this gourd bowl by pressing small beads into warm beeswax.

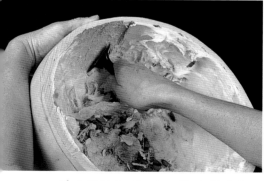

Photo 9. Notice the nice white inside lining in this big gourd. Keep slices of it to use in projects. Use proper tools and wear a dust mask when cleaning the inside of a gourd.

CLEANING THE INSIDE

What you have at this point is a gourd that is clean on the outside surface, cut open in some way and showing an assortment of seeds and pulp on the inside. Now you have to remove this material to reveal the smooth interior gourd wall. Some gourds are almost self-cleaning. There is a ball of seeds and pulp that merely falls out when the gourd is overturned. This is called a good gourd day. More often, we find the seeds and membrane stuck to the inside wall. It's still a good gourd day, it's just more challenging!

Cleaning the inside of dried gourds is a dusty endeavor, so it's a good idea to work outdoors if weather permits. Indoors or out, wear a dust mask or use a respirator, and wear safety glasses. You'll need several tools to clean the wide variety of gourd sizes you'll want to use. (See photo 8.)

Tools for Cleaning the Insides of Gourds

Scraper, a curved blade with a short handle

Extra long needle-nose pliers

Variable speed power drill, cordless or plug-in

Mounted wire brushes in a variety of sizes and shapes

¼-inch (6 mm) diameter shank extension in two lengths: 6 inches (15.2 cm) and 12 inches (30.5 cm)

Half-round file (cabinet maker's file is best)

Sandpaper, in 100,120,150,180, and 220 grit

Dust mask

Safety glasses

Several small pebbles

For larger openings, such as bowls, you'll need to completely clean the inside. Empty any loose material first, and then scrape the inside surface. Sometimes it's necessary to score the white shiny inside skin with a series of vertical cuts, using a corner of the scraper. (See Photo 9.) Be careful not to scratch too deeply. Then scrape the whole area again with the convex side of the scraper.

If the opening cut is narrow, the gourd will be next to impossible to thoroughly clean. In such gourds, just pay attention to the part of the interior that's visible. Scrape and sand to the extent you can reach. Empty out any seeds and pulp. Use a long rod or screwdriver to help break up any stuck areas. Place a few small pebbles in the gourd and shake gently to help loosen the pulp from the sides.

I've had success using a ¼" (6.35 mm) shank, mounted wire brushes used in a cordless or power drill. (See photo 10.) These come in a variety of sizes and shapes. Use a low rpm and light pressure to avoid cutting into the wall of the gourd. Drill extensions that accept ¼" (6.35 mm) shanks allow for deep work. These are commonly available in 6-inch and 12-inch (15.2 and 30.5 cm) lengths.

Dump out the gourd frequently and inspect your progress. Use sandpaper to obtain the smoothest surface. Start with 100 grit and proceed through finer grits. Usually 150 grit is enough, but for food containers, even 220 grit may be needed. Lastly, ease the inside edge with sandpaper. The inside should be as neat and clean as the outside.

Wet Soaking

One of the advantages of the wet soaking method is that there's no dust. It works best when you soak several gourds at the same time. First, fill the gourds with water. Let them soak overnight. Some gourds may take several days to soak. The idea is to soften the inside material and then pull or scrape it out. The cleaned gourd has to dry thoroughly before you can do any crafting on the outside, so schedule accordingly.

FINISHING THE INTERIOR

How you finish the interior of your gourd often depends on whether or not you want it to be a container for food. If the gourd is not intended for food, you can finish the interior any way you'd like.

If you intend to use the gourd for liquids or food and want to keep it totally natural, here's how. Clean the gourd thoroughly and sand it smooth. Then, fill it with water, let it stand a day or two, and rinse with fresh water. If the water has a bitter taste, repeat the process, adding a few tablespoons of sodium bicarbonate. How many times you need to repeat the soak and rinse process will depend on the individual gourd. Let the gourd dry thoroughly.

For use with such items as buttery rolls and popcorn, you'll want a protective layer on the inside of the gourd. Any product that is formulated for safe use with wooden food preparation items, such as wooden bowls, spoons, and cutting boards is fine for use with gourds. This would include such products as nut oils and mineral oil. Always check the label and follow the manufacturer's recommendations.

Design Tips

To give my art pieces an attractive background contrast to their outside colors, I use a flat black enamel spray paint on the insides. I've recommended this technique in the project instructions.

Photo 10. Use a power drill with a stainless steel brush on an extension to clean inside tall, narrow gourds.

Design Tips

Some gourds have an inside "knob" on the center of the bottom, where the blossom once was. This can be snapped off using long-nose pliers.

Judy Mofield Mallow, *Sacred Objects Around the Year*, 1999, gourd bottom with bead and pine needle insert, pine needle rim. Figures painted in acrylic paint by Bruce Stiles. Photo by McKenzie Photography

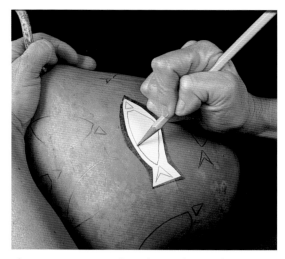

Photo 11. It's easy and quick to make template patterns and transfer them to the surface of the gourd. The templates for fourteen projects are in the back of the book, starting on page 120.

This lively lady from Colombia is made entirely from gourds and colored with acrylic paint. Virginia Saunders collection

DECORATING THE OUTSIDE OF THE GOURD

All the prep work leads up to the fun part of gourdcrafting—decorating the outside of the gourd. Like all artistic techniques, gourd decorating takes practice, so be patient with yourself. In this section I explain the most basic gourdcrafting techniques such as transferring a template, adding color, pyrography, and carving. In some of the projects, such as the Rice Bowl with Chopsticks project on page 58. I introduce you to some specific new techniques.

Transferring a Template

The projects in this book have designs that you can trace onto the gourds. Do this by reducing or enlarging the templates, as needed, on a copy machine. Cut out the design on the paper, but leave a small border around it, so you can easily trace the pattern and not lose its lines. Position a piece of transfer paper under the pattern. Use clear transparent tape to hold the pattern and the transfer paper onto the desired section of the gourd.

With a pencil, lightly trace the pattern onto the gourd. (See photo 11.) After you have finished tracing, remove the pattern and transfer paper and darken any undefined lines with the pencil.

Adding Color

One of the most exciting features of gourd art is that you can use an incredibly wide range of media to color the gourds. I know for sure that two artists faced with the same gourd would choose different color media. I have friends who work successfully with water-soluble felt pens, shoe cream (which can be purchased in a wide variety of colors including silver, copper and gold metallics), wood stains, opaque water-soluble acrylics, oil pastels, silk painting dyes, colored inks, waxed crayon, spray paint, tempera paints, oil paints, water color paints, textured paints, metallic gold and copper pens, metallic finishes, and powders. Most colorants are not colorfast. So if you put your gourd in direct sunlight, its colors will fade (not to mention that the gourd might crack, too).

Coloring with Leather Dyes

My choice is leather dyes, also known as *spirit dyes*. Leather dye is a transparent medium, relying for most of its effects on the fact that the rays of light penetrate the color on the gourd and are reflected back to the viewer through the transparent film of the dye. The transparent colors allow the natural colors and textures of the gourd to show through. The dye absorbs into the shell, creating a rich leather-like appearance. Leather dyes, most of which are alcohol-based, are permanent. Isopropyl alcohol can remove some dye, but usually not all of it.

Artists who have never used leather dyes are amazed to discover how easy they are to work with and how few tools you really need. (See photo 12.)

Tools for Applying Leather Dyes

Foam brushes, usually 1-inch (2.5) wide

Artist's paintbrushes, usually size 4 flat shader

Daubers, or cotton swabs

Protective gloves

When applying dyes, don't load up your brushes. A little goes a long way. The color is permanent, so wear gloves when using the dye; if you're sensitive to latex, choose vinyl gloves.

When leather dye is applied to a hard, smooth surface, it will run; on a porous surface, it quickly penetrates. A smooth shell may require one or two coats of dye. On a porous surface one coat will usually be sufficient. Successive coats will produce darker shades.

You can purchase leather dyes from leather supply companies, shoe repair shops, some art supply stores, and on the Internet. They come in 4-ounce (.12 L) and one-quart (.9 L) bottles. Gather a supply of wonderful short, fat jars that won't get knocked over easily, and transfer your dyes into them.

Leather dyes are available in a wide range of colors, most of which look absolutely terrific on gourds, such as chocolate, dark brown, medium brown, light brown, mahogany, British tan (which is a beautiful rust color), tan, buckskin, red, yellow, light blue, oxblood (dark red), orange, aqua green, russet, and black. There are two colors I don't recommend: navy blue tends to be too dark, and white just doesn't show up.

Design Tips

Mix dyes to create different hues. Mix them in a separate container, or lay one color over another directly onto the gourd. Use a scrap piece of gourd (preferably from the same gourd) to experiment with mixing colors and work out the right proportions for the effects you want. For example, to make a red a deeper, richer shade, just add a few drops of mahogany.

Photo 12. Leather dyes come in a wonderful variety of colors. Apply the dye with foam brushes, artist paintbrushes, daubers, or cotton swabs.

Dyan Mai Peterson, *Spots*, 1997, leather dyes, devil's claw seedpod, reed, gold thread, coin, beads. Photo by Tim Barnwell

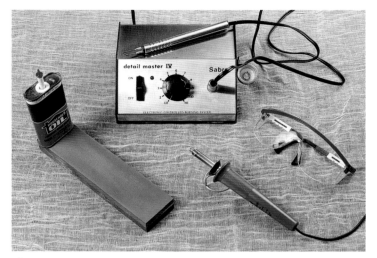

Photo 14. Pyrography tools; clockwise: burning system with a variable heat regulator (my recommendation); self-contained burning pen; sharpening stone and oil

Pyrography

Pyrography (or pyro-engraving) is the art of producing a design using a heated tool. Some people refer to it as woodburning, but when burning gourds we call it pyrography. The results achieved with pyrography depend on the type of gourd, the shape of the burning tip, and range of temperatures, speed, and pressure you use. Gourd skins that are soft (usually light in color) will burn quickly, while gourds with hard, dense skins may require a higher burning temperature, more pressure, and a slower pulling speed.

Heat recovery is the ability of the burning tool to re-attain its starting heat after it's been used for a while. Heat recovery varies from model to model in pyrography tools, and is dependent on wattage; the lower the wattage, the longer the heat recovery time, hence the longer it takes to burn because of the time spent waiting for the tool to reheat.

Basically there are two types of pyrography tools on the market today that are appropriate for the projects in this book: a self-contained burning pen and a burning system. (See photo 14.) Each tool has several burning tips available for every kind of use, which you can easily keep sharp with a sharpening stone.

The *self-contained burning* pens are readily available at craft supply and hobby stores. The heating element is in the hand-held unit itself. Heat recovery will be slow due to the low wattage. Even so, good work can be produced at an affordable price.

The *burning system* consists of solid-state electronic circuitry with a variable heat regulator dial and an on/off switch, all contained in a steel control box, which sits on your workbench. *Burning pens* come in a wide variety of burning tips and plug into the unit. You hold the tip as you would hold a writing pen, which makes it relatively easy to control. The ideal burning system has a unit of 100 watts or more. It can be dialed to reach a temperature as high as 2,000°F (1,093°C) in seven seconds. Just as important, it also stays at the temperature you dial, which means you can keep a constant high temperature for hard skin gourds and an equally constant lower temperature for soft skin gourds. When you're burning a long line, the constancy of the temperature gives you more control.

Photo 15. To create straight, clean burn lines, you need to keep your burning tip sharp.

Design Tips

Practice and experiment with different burning tips, as each tip is capable of many different effects. Save your experimental gourd scraps as a reference. You may also want to label each test effort, noting which tip was used.

For the projects in this book, you need learn only two pyrography techniques and use only one burning tip. The techniques are burning straight lines and simple curved lines. The burning tip is a general duty straight-tip that is designed to burn straight lines. Always keep your burning tip sharp. A dull burning tip will drag and create thick, uneven lines. Follow the manufacturer's advice on sharpening and caring for your burning tips. Work in a well-ventilated area. If you are sensitive to smoke, wear a respirator mask.

For *straight lines*, I prefer a thin, crisp line just deep enough to act as a reservoir to hold the leather dye. When burning a straight line, maintain an even rate of speed as you pull the pen toward you along the design line. (See photo 15 on page 22.)

Curved lines are more difficult to produce than straight lines, so they will require more practice. Make curves by rotating the gourd and move the burning tip in the opposite direction. When burning a small, tight radius, turn the temperature down low, rotate the gourd, and lightly burn in the curve. Next, turn up the temperature and reburn until the curve is dark enough.

Before burning in the lines of the pattern, practice burning straight lines on a gourd scrap, preferably the top portion of the gourd you just cut off. This scrap is invaluable for testing because it will be of the same character as your project piece. (This also applies for testing dyes, paints, etc.) When you've become acquainted with your burning tool, you'll have enough experience to determine the temperature at which to burn, and also the speed.

Carving

Carving is the process of removing areas of the outer hard skin of the gourd, revealing the lovely white or cream-colored lining underneath, and giving color contrast and texture to your design. A medium- to thick-walled gourd is best for carving. There are two types of carving tools, which differ greatly in cost and efficiency. (See photo 16.)

A *cordless rotary carving tool* (with two speeds and a three-hour battery charger) is ideal if you do very little carving, or haven't decided yet how much time and money you want to invest in carving tools. It's a great starter tool and when I was beginning to learn how to carve, it provided satisfactory results. As you gain more experience, however, you may find it to be a bit clumsy and tiring, as I did.

What works best for me now is a *1/8 HP motor that hangs from a hook* on a pole clamped to my workbench. A *flexible shaft* goes from the motor over my shoulder to a handpiece with a collet that accepts various burs. I also use an electronic *foot pedal*, which frees my hands for better control while carving. It also gives me an extra punch of high speed any time I need it, giving me infinitely sensitive motor control capabilities from zero rpm to the maximum speed of the motor.

Dyan Mai Peterson, *Going to Market*, 2001, carved, pyrography, leather dyes, oak handle wrapped with waxed linen thread and reed. Photo by Evan Bracken

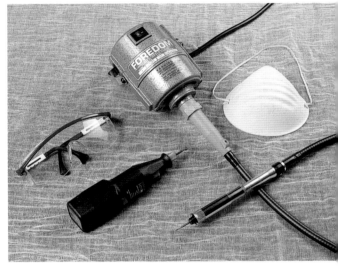

Photo 16. A simple cordless rotary tool (lower left) is great for beginning gourd carvers. For extensive and efficient carving, consider using the more powerful hanging motor with a long flexible shaft. (upper right)

There are two different carving techniques: *Bas-relief* is the removal of the background, so the design of the darker skin is more prominent. The *incision technique* cuts a design into the hardshell so the lighter underskin forms the lines of the design. We use both methods in the projects in the book, sometimes in the same project. The truth is, I enjoy carving so much that almost every project has some carving in it.

Burs come in all shapes and sizes, each having its own purpose; they also come in different materials, ranging from tungsten vanadium (which is the least hard and also inexpensive) to diamond carbide (which is the hardest and most expensive, but worth it). To simplify the techniques in the book, however, I used only two types of burs: *a cylinder square cross-cut bur* with a 3/32-inch (2.38 mm) shank and 1/16-inch (1.44 mm) diameter cylinder, and a *round ball bur* with a 3/32-inch (2.38 mm) shank and a 3/16-inch (4.7 mm) diameter ball.

Photo 17. When using the bas-relief technique, work one small section at a time and use a steady even pressure.

The *cylinder square cross-cut bur* will allow you to carve short straight lines, swirls, squares, little dots, cross-hatching, and other shapes. Use this bur to sign your name and date your work on the bottom of your gourds.

The *round ball bur*, as the name implies, makes round dots (seen in many projects throughout the book) and is used in the bas-relief technique (see photo 17), which is described in detail in the Carved Flower Vase project on page 56.

Once you've learned the techniques with these two burs, purchases other burs of different shapes and sizes and experiment with them on pieces of gourd. (See the carving sampler on the opposite page.) Save your test pieces for reference, noting which bur was used with each test.

Very important: Always keep in mind that gourds have a round surface and the bur rotates in a circular motion, so it can easily run off the surface. Therefore, keep the hand holding the gourd out of direct line of the bur in case it should slip. Always wear a dust mask and safety glasses.

FINISHING THE EXTERIOR

There are many options available for protective gourd coatings, such as polyurethane, lacquer varnishes, shellac, wood sealers, and waxes. Whatever finish you choose, it must be compatible with your color medium. I prefer a spray lacquer (with a clear matte or semi-gloss finish), which enhances the color of the leather dyes I use, while bringing out the textures and colors of the gourd skin. It provides much-needed protection from splattered water, is easy to apply, and quick to dry (a real advantage when you are coloring many items at one time).

When you spray, work outdoors or in a well-ventilated room, follow the manufacturer's directions on the can, and wear a

Dyan Mai Peterson, *One Stick*, 1999, carved with incision technique, pyrography, leather dyes, boiled grapevine handle. Photo by Tim Barnwell

protective mask. Don't be heavy handed with the spray. Spray a fine mist, a little at a time, and let it dry thoroughly. A hair dryer, on a low setting, is so helpful to speed up drying that I've listed it as an essential tool in the projects. One coat should be sufficient for most projects, but if you want to add a second finely misted coat for extra protection, go ahead. Be especially gentle when spraying designs made with felt-tip pens, which will run if the spray is too thick.

Gourds have some of the same characteristics as wood. They expand and contract with the moisture in the air. Finished gourds, like wood, should not be placed in a sunny window or left in the sun. The moisture in the gourd wall can evaporate and cause the gourd to crack. Sun also fades the color. Handle gourds carefully, lifting them from their bottoms, rather than from their rims.

Create a beautiful carving sampler gourd by experimenting with different kinds of cutting burs.

Repairing Blemishes and Cracks

As gifts of nature, gourds come to us with all kinds of natural imperfections, such as marks from growing, or damage caused by insects. I see these imperfections as part of the beauty and character of the gourd and try to incorporate them into my design. A gourd with a lot of dents and holes makes a perfect design surface for a mask, for example.

But if you find that a damaged or irregular area is interfering with your design, you can easily fix that. Apply wood putty with a putty knife to the area, smooth out the putty, and let it dry. Gently sand the repair with 150-grit sandpaper. Repeat the process as needed to obtain a smooth surface.

Use the same technique to repair a crack on the gourd. First, however, you must drill a small hole at both ends of the crack to prevent the crack from spreading any further. Then apply the putty with a putty knife and smooth it. (See photo 18.) Cracks can also be repaired with a stitching or lacing method, similar to tying your shoes with laces, and be incorporated into the design as an embellishment. Many different types of threads, cords, and leather may be used. See the Warm-Glow Lampshade project on page 70, in which I deliberately created a crack on the rim of a gourd as part of my overall design.

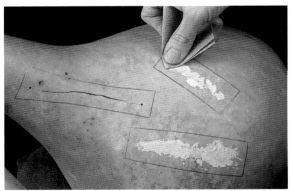

Photo 18. A crack in the gourd skin isn't a disaster. Drill two holes on either end of the crack to keep it from spreading, cover it with putty, then sand it smooth.

Leveling the Bottom of the Gourd

There are several methods to stabilize a gourd bottom so it stands in the proper position. You can level the bottom by sanding down the high points with a sanding block. You can also add gourd scrap or a foot to the low point to keep it in an upright position.

Feet look best on gourds when they are either inconspicuous or part of the design. I prefer to make the feet out of natural materials that complement and embellish the gourd, such as sticks, bamboo, seashells, or clay beads. A woven wreath makes a wonderful pedestal or "nest." I also make "ring feet" from slices of the handle of a dipper gourd. Sand or bevel the edge of the rings to fit the contour of the bottom of the gourd.

Adding a Stem

A gourd stem adds a finishing touch to a project, especially to an uncut gourd or one with a lid. If the stem of your gourd is missing or broken, you can easily replace it with the stem from another gourd.

Locate a stem that will be in the appropriate proportion to your gourd. Position the stem on the gourd where it will look its best, then clean both the stem and the area on the gourd that will be near it. To attach the stem to the gourd, you'll need a toothpick, wooden shish kabob skewer, or small round basket reed as a support. Drill a hole in the gourd and also into the stem. The size of the hole you drill will be determined by what type and size of support material you are using. Drill the hole as deep as you can, preferably $\frac{1}{2}$ inch (1.3 cm) into the stem base end and $\frac{1}{2}$ inch (1.3 cm) into the gourd. The deeper the holes, the stronger the stem will be. Be careful not to drill all the way through the stem or gourd. Cut the support to desired length. Add a few drops of quick-set epoxy glue into the holes in the gourd and the stem, and insert the support into both holes. (See photo 19.) Make adjustments if needed. Let the glue dry thoroughly.

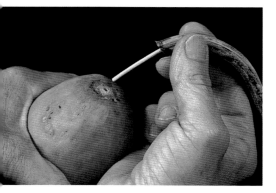

Photo 19. Simple drilling, glueing, and some touch-up coloring will repair or replace a lost stem.

To blend the stem into the gourd, dye the stem the same color as the surrounding area. Use wood putty to fill in any undesirable gaps. Although this stem should be stronger than the original was, handle it with care.

EMBELLISHMENT

An embellishment is something decorative added to the gourd. It can be as simple as a string of gourd seeds added as a final touch, or be the focus of the piece, such as the wild decorations on masks. With embellishments, the only tools you need to attach them are an awl or drill and some thread. You can use just about anything to embellish a gourd.

Each project in the book has embellishments, such as bamboo, buttons, basket reed, and lots of beads. Since gourds are natural to begin with, I prefer natural embellishments to complement them. Be gourd-minded when you're out in nature and keep your eyes open for such found treasures as seeds, nuts and pods, sticks, feathers, dried berries, acorns, driftwood, and seashells.

Dyan Mai Peterson, *Working the Earth*, 2000, pyrography, carved, leather dye, rim treatment of palm influorescence, embroidery thread, beads. Photo by Evan Bracken

RIM TREATMENTS

A rim treatment is an embellishment specifically on the rim of a cut gourd. Rim treatments can be as simple as a sandpaper-smoothed rim or as elaborate as coiled rows of pine needles. I almost always add rim treatments as part of my design, but I prefer to keep them simple and use natural materials to harmonize with the artwork on the body of the gourds. In the projects with rim treatments in the book, I've given detailed instructions on how to make them, using such items as pine needles, basket reed, and grapevine. Other materials you could use include such wonderful natural things as honeysuckle vines, willow bark, sugar palm fiber, sweet grass, hemp, horsehair, and handspun yarns. Also notice the gourds in the gallery, for almost all of them have rim treatments of some kind.

ABOUT THE PROJECTS

Gourd art by its nature is one of the most flexible creative endeavors. Some projects can be done quickly with the barest expenditure of time and tools. Others expand in stages, with a variety of techniques and equipment, and require the fine and often forgotten art of patience. Fast or slow, all the projects in the book are relatively easy to make. You'll find some traditional techniques, such as carving and pyrography, which are fundamental to gourd craft. In addition, I've offered several new techniques that I hope will be innovative for even experienced gourd artists.

Dyan Mai Peterson, *Hold This, Hide That*, 2000, carved, pyrography, leather dye. Walnut stand with drawer by Gary Peterson. Photo by Evan Bracken

In each project you'll find a list of all the materials you'll need to make it. Listed first is the specific type of gourd, and any other natural materials you might need to gather. Then the other materials are listed in the way they're called for in the instructions. In the tools and supplies section, the first things listed are the type(s) of saw you'll need for the project as well as any electric tools, including the hair dryer used for drying the leather dyes. These are followed by the other tool and supply items in order of their use. The step-by-step instructions take you from the cutting of a cleaned gourd all the way through to the final embellishments. (Of course, remember to clean the inside of each gourd and let it dry after you cut it, as described on page 18.) The project templates are listed together in the back of the book, starting on page 120.

After you've gained some experience, I hope you'll follow my primary piece of advice—use your own imagination and create your own design style. As I'm sure you can understand, the designs in the book are for your personal use only, or to give away as presents to your loved ones. Since my livelihood comes from creating and selling my art, please be respectful of my request that you not reproduce these projects for commercial use or juried exhibitions.

May all your days be Gourd Days!

Whimsical

BEADED GOURD-IN-ORBIT

Take a creative whirl with this wild, yet oh-so-easy-to-make bowl. Simple spirals of basket reed and colorful beads create the spinning orbit effect. Launch a truly galactic impression with a display of several gourds and lots of different beads.

Materials

- Gourd with a shape suitable to go in orbit, cleaned
- #3 round basket reed, 3 yards (2.7 m) long
- Flat black enamel spray paint
- Leather dyes: light brown, black
- Clear satin lacquer spray finish
- Cylindrical beads (with holes large enough to fit on the reed)
- Quick-set epoxy glue

Tools and Supplies

- Small precision jigsaw or handsaw (see page 15)
- Hair dryer
- Pyrography tool with straight-line burning tip
- Power drill with bits appropriate to the size holes of your beads
- 100-grit sandpaper
- 1-inch (2.5 cm) foam brush
- Pencil
- Small artist paintbrush, size 4 flat shader
- Round file (optional)
- Measuring tape
- Scissors

Cutting and Coloring the Gourd and Reed

1. Use the straight-cut technique described on page 17 to cut off the top of the gourd.

2. Clean, sand, and spray the inside of the gourd with the black enamel paint.

3. Use the foam brush to coat the exterior of the gourd with the light brown dye. Allow the dye to dry completely, using the hair dryer to speed the drying if you wish.

4. Dye the basket reed with the black dye and allow it to dry. Set it aside for now.

Decorating the Gourd

5. Using the pencil, draw horizontal lines around the gourd (the number of lines will depend on the size of your gourd). Then draw vertical lines to create boxes.

Don't worry about being too finicky. All the lines can be fluid. See the photo for guidance.

6. Use the straight-line burning tip to burn in all the lines you drew.

7. Use the small paintbrush and black dye to darken the band at the top and outline the boxes. Dry it with the hair dryer.

8. To seal the gourd and protect your work, apply a fine mist of clear satin lacquer spray finish, and allow it to dry.

9. Select a drill bit that is slightly smaller than the outside diameter of the beads you have chosen, and drill a hole in the center of each box on the gourd.

10. If necessary, use a round file to open the holes just enough for the beads to fit in. Put the epoxy glue on each bead and push it into a hole, so that about half of the bead is sticking out from the surface of the gourd. Put beads into all the boxes and allow them the glue to set.

11. Soak the reed in water for about five minutes or until it becomes flexible.

12. Select two beads on the gourd for spanning a strip of reed. Use the measuring tape to find out the distance between the beads, adding 1 inch (2.5 cm) or more for the curvature of the reed. Use the scissors to cut off a piece of reed slightly longer than this length. Insert the reed into the center of the beads and trim it, if needed.

13. Continue to add pieces of reed all around the gourd until the gourd looks complete enough to launch into display mode. Using the same techniques, you could make a gourd orbit big enough for a buffet table centerpiece or tiny enough to twirl from the chandelier.

Gourdian Angel

~

Perfectly beautiful wings are made from a unique cloud-like material—the white inside lining scraped carefully from a big gourd. The pretty angel is so much fun to make, you'll be tempted to create an entire heavenly choir!

Materials

- Small gourd with neck, cleaned
- Egg gourd, cleaned
- Large piece of the white inside lining of a large gourd
- Leather dyes: buckskin, light brown
- Quick-set epoxy glue
- Pastel matte beads (enough for halo and necklace)
- Needle
- Thread

Tools and Supplies

- Hacksaw
- Hair dryer
- 1-inch (2.5 cm) foam brush
- Paper towels

Cutting and Coloring the Angel Body

1. Use the hacksaw and the angle-cut technique described on page 17 to cut off the top of the small gourd.

2. With the foam brush apply buckskin leather dye to the gourd.

3. While the buckskin dye is still moist, apply light brown dye to the top 1-inch (2.5 cm) edge of the gourd. Using a paper towel, blend the light brown dye down and into the buckskin dye. This shading method gives the angel dimension. Dry it with the hair dryer.

4. Color the egg gourd with buckskin dye and dry it with the hair dryer, too.

Making the Wings and the Collar

5. From the piece of white inner lining from another gourd, tear two pieces into the shapes of wings, appropriately sized to the body of the angel. Bend the bottom portions of the wing back and flat to create a glue surface.

6. Glue one of the wings onto the gourd. Hold the wing in place for a minute while the glue is setting. Then glue on the second wing.

7. Tear two small pieces of white gourd lining to resemble a collar, and glue them onto the top edge of the neck of the gourd.

Making the Head and Halo

8. Create a necklace by stringing beads with needle and thread and tie a knot. The length of the necklace should be appropriate to the size of the angel's body.

9. Placing it at a slight angle (which looks better than straight up), glue the egg gourd in place for the angel's head. Let it dry.

10. Make a beaded halo. Glue it to the head and let it dry thoroughly. To use the angel as a tree topper, just drill a hole in the bottom of the gourd that is big enough for the top tree branch and slip the angel into place.

BEADED MASK

Magical and mysterious, masks are my favorite art pieces. When you wear a mask people wonder—who is that being hiding behind it? Or, as mask performers say, put on a mask and reveal more of you. With color, wire, and beads, a simple gourd mask becomes an object of daring imagination.

Materials

Kettle gourd, cleaned

Mask template, page 122

Transparent tape

Transfer paper

Flat black enamel spray paint

Leather dyes: medium brown, buckskin, British tan, aqua green, black

Clear satin lacquer spray finish

18-gauge (1.00 mm) wire, about 8 feet (2.43 m) in length

Assortment of large and medium-sized beads

Tools and Supplies

Power drill with 3/32-inch (2.38 mm) drill bit

Small precision jigsaw or handsaw (see page 15)

Pyrography tool with straight-line burning tip

Hair dryer

Carving tool with cylinder square cross-cut bur (optional) (see page 24)

Pencil

150-grit sandpaper

Utility knife (optional)

1-inch (2.5 cm) foam brushes

Cotton swabs

Wire cutters

Round-nose pliers (optional)

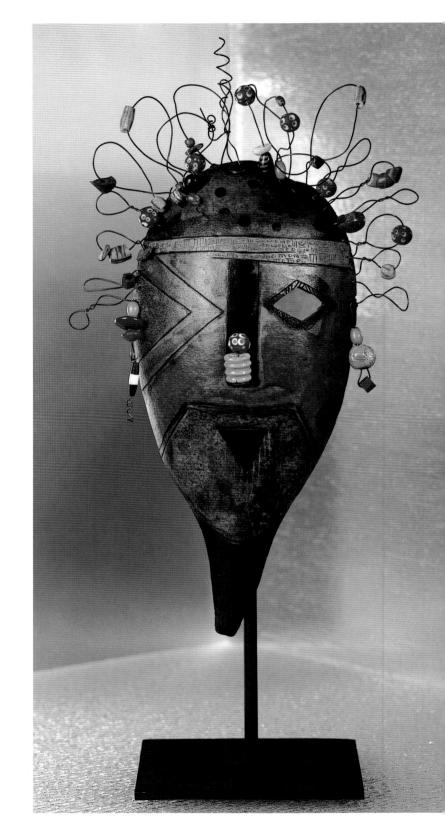

Making the Mask

1. Tape the transfer paper to the gourd and use the pencil to trace the mask template on page 122 onto the curved contours of the gourd. If your mask will be a wall decoration, it can be any size you want. If you want to wear it, make it a size that will be comfortable for you to wear.

2. Drill a small hole in the gourd at any point just outside the pencil line of the perimeter of the mask. Insert the saw blade into the hole to get your cutting line going, and cut the mask out of the gourd.

3. Clean and sand the back of the mask so it will be smooth and pleasant to wear against your face. (And so it'll look nice even if you're going to hang it. People always peek at the back of a mask.) Spray with the black paint and let it dry.

5. Following the pencil lines inside your design, outline the lines with the straight-line burning tip. If you intend to wear the mask, cut out the eyes with the utility knife. (Or do what I do because I think it looks more mysterious—cut out only one eye.)

6. With a foam brush, apply the dyes to color various portions of the face. Dye the area around the mouth with medium brown dye, and sand it lightly with the sandpaper to create an antique effect. Hasten the drying between applications by blowing the dyed areas with the hair dryer. If you wish, use a cotton swab to add black dots of dye to the forehead.

7. Color the headband on the forehead. Or do what I did, and add texture by burning and carving in small squares, circles, and lines.

8. Spray a coat of clear satin lacquer spray finish over the entire mask and allow it to dry thoroughly.

Attaching the Wire

9. Starting at the center of the right eye, no less than ¼ inch (6 mm) from the edge of the mask, drill holes about ½ inch (1.3 cm) apart around the edge of the mask, all the way to the opposite side.

10. With the wire cutters, cut off a piece of wire about 8 feet (2.4 m) long. Insert the wire into the second hole, twist it into a whimsical, untamed-hair

shape, add a bead or two, and insert it into the third hole. If needed, use the round-nose pliers to help. (Leave the first and last holes empty for now; you'll put the earrings there in the next step.) Repeat until you have filled the holes around the head of the mask. Have fun twisting the wire and adding the beads— the wilder the better.

11. Stack beads onto a couple short pieces of wire to simulate earrings, and twist the wire to hold the beads in place. Insert into the first and last holes.

12. Add a finishing touch by decorating the nose. Drill holes in the top and bottom of the nose. Place a couple beads on a short length of wire, insert the ends into the holes, and twist them together on the back to hold them in place.

13. If you want to hang your mask, secure a length of wire across the back.

14. Admire your mask on the wall—or put it over your face and look in a mirror and be amazed by the creation that looks back at you.

Dyan Mai Peterson, (left) *Breathe In, Breathe Out*, 2000, pyrography, leather dyes, driftwood, waxed linen thread, wire, reed, paper and beads, (right) *Breathing Companion*, 2000, pyrography, leather dyes, beads, wire, carved nest egg lid. Photo by Evan Bracken

Miniature Gourd Martin House

I love watching the purple martins return every spring and take up residency in the big gourd martin houses in my backyard. I created this miniature replica, made of small ornamental gourds, to capture the essence of spring all year long.

Materials

7 small ornamental gourds for the birdhouses, cleaned

1 block of wood, 1¾ x 3½ x 3½ inches (4.4 x 8.9 x 8.9 cm)

2 sticks in proportion to the gourds you are using. (The sticks I used were 9 inches and 18 inches (22.9 cm and 45.7 cm) long.)

Raffia

Quick-set epoxy glue

Raffia

Quick-set epoxy glue

Tools and Supplies

Power drill with bits suitable for the stick and the size of the gourds

Making the Stick Support

1. Drill a hole in the center of the block of wood. Insert the longest stick into the hole. This should be a tight fit.

2. Glue the stick into the hole and let it dry.

3. Use the raffia to tie the shorter stick horizontally onto the first stick.

Making the Birdhouses

4. Six of the seven birdhouses will hang from the support stick. The other you'll use as decoration at the top. Drill entrance holes into all the gourds. The entrance holes should be in proportion to the size of the gourds. Use whatever size drill bit is suitable.

5. Make the hangers one at a time for the six gourds that will hang from the support stick. Drill a hole into one side of a gourd near the top and through to the other side. Repeat for the remaining five birdhouses that will hang.

6. Tear pieces of raffia into thin strips and insert them in the holes on the tops of the birdhouses. Then tie them onto the stick and secure them with knots.

7. To keep the birdhouses from rotating, tie more strips of raffia onto the raffia hangers, just below the horizontal stick. Use the photo of the project for guidance.

8. In the bottom of the last birdhouse, drill a hole large enough for the stick to enter. Add a touch of glue to secure it in place. Place the martin house near a window, so when you look past it to the outdoors, it feels as if you are bringing nature inside.

Dyan Mai Peterson, *The Biggest Birdhouse You Ever Saw*, 1999, pyrography, leather dye, carved. Photo by Evan Bracken

HELMET-HEADED GOURDRUNNER

Allow your imagination to take flight with this wacky bird and her cargo of colorful eggs. Just combine gourd parts and decorate them in wild ways. Once you've made one gourdrunner, you'll discover the same secret I did—it's even more fun to make a whole flock.

Materials

- 3 ornamental nest egg gourds for the pedestal (small, medium, and large), cleaned
- Ornamental gourd in the shape of the bird body, with its stem suitable for the bird beak, cleaned
- Gourd scraps suitable for the wings, cleaned
- Small ornamental banana gourd for the bird's helmet, cleaned
- Round basket reed, size # 3, 2 inches (5 cm) long, or toothpicks
- Wooden dowel, 1/4 inch (6 mm) in diameter, 10 inches (25.4 cm) long
- Flat black enamel spray paint
- Block of wood, 1 1/2 x 3 x 3 inches (3.8 x 7.6 x 7.6 cm)
- Wood stain, brown
- Quick-set epoxy glue
- Leather dyes: light brown, medium brown, black, aqua green
- Clear satin lacquer spray finish
- 18-gauge (1.00 mm) copper wire, 36 inches (.91 m) long
- 2 copper nails

Tools and Supplies

- Power drill with 1/4-inch (6.35 mm) and 3/32-inch (2.38 mm) drill bits
- Pyrography tool with straight-line burning tip
- Carving tool with both a cylinder square cross-cut bur and a round ball bur (see page 24)
- Hair dryer
- Handsaw
- Pencil
- Cotton swabs
- 1-inch (2.5 cm) foam brush
- 150-grit sandpaper
- Scissors
- Awl
- Utility knife

Making the Pedestal

1. Spray the dowel with flat black enamel spray paint. Let it dry.

2. Dye the block of wood with the brown wood stain. Let it dry.

3. Drill a hole in the center of the block of wood. Glue the dowel into the hole and allow it to dry.

Making the Eggs

4. Dye the large and medium nest egg gourds light brown; dye the small nest egg gourd medium brown.

5. Decorate the large and medium eggs first. With the pencil, draw small abstract and geometric shapes on the large nest egg gourd. On the medium nest egg gourd, draw squares of various sizes with over-lapping lines.

6. Use the straight-line burning tip to burn in all the layout lines on the two gourds. Color in the shapes with black dye.

7. Now decorate the small egg. Dip a cotton swab in black dye and create a dot pattern on its surface.

8. Spray all three eggs with clear satin lacquer spray finish.

9. Use the round ball bur to carve in decorative dots on the black dyed areas of all three eggs.

10. Drill a 1/4-inch (6 mm) hole through the center of each egg. Slide the eggs onto the dowel. (See the photo.)

Making the Bird

11. Decorate the neck of the ornamental gourd you've selected for the bird body by pencil drawing three rings around the gourd. Space them approximately 1/4 to 3/8 inch (6 to 9.5 mm) apart. Use a cotton swab dipped in black dye to color them. Dry with the hair dryer. Use aqua green dye to fill in between the black rings.

12. Use the foam brush and light brown dye to color all the remaining areas of the bird. Dry with the hair dryer.

13. Use a cotton swab and black dye to create dots for the eyes and to color the beak made of the gourd stem. Spray the whole bird with clear satin lacquer spray finish.

14. Use a round ball bur to carve the eyes and make decorative dots on the neck.

Making the Wings

15. From the gourd scraps, cut two wing shapes in proportion to the bird's body. Gently sand the edges.

16. With a cotton swab, dye the wing tip with aqua green dye. Dye the edge of the aqua green area with black dye. Dye the remainder of the wing with light brown dye. Repeat this color process on the second wing.

17. Decorate the brown area of the wings with shapes and techniques used on the nest egg gourds. Dry with the hair dryer. Spray the wings with a coat of clear satin lacquer spray finish. Then carve the dots on them and set them aside. Because the wings will protrude from the body a bit, you don't want to attach them now and risk damaging them while you work on the rest of the bird. You'll add them as the next-to-last step.

Making the Helmet

18. To make the helmet, use the handsaw to cut off the top 2-inch (5 cm) section of the banana gourd.

Double-Duty Birdhouse

This woven birdhouse serves double duty. It provides a whimsical way to help wild birds easily find nesting materials. And then when they've taken all the materials, what remains is a birdhouse they can live in! First wrap a grapevine frame around a suitably sized, cleaned gourd. Then random weave around it, using natural materials, such as 100 percent prewashed cotton twine, natural fibers such as grapevine, honeysuckle, and gourd vines, twigs, grasses—anything you can weave. This gives the birds a wide variety of nesting materials to choose from. It's important to use all natural fibers in such a structure because baby birds may ingest the materials in the nest the mother birds make, and birds can't digest synthetic fibers such as polyester, nylon, rayon, etc. Customize your birdhouse with the proper entrance hole to accommodate the species you are trying to attract. Hang the birdhouse in the correct habitat. To save the gourd and keep next year's inhabitants healthy, take your birdhouse down in the fall, clean it and store until the next spring.

19. Dye the helmet light brown, and make black dots with a cotton swab. Let it dry. Spray with clear satin lacquer spray finish.

20. With the scissors, cut two 1-inch (2.5 cm) lengths of the basket reed and dye them black. Dry them with the hair dryer.

21. Position the helmet onto the bird's head. Hold it in place while you attach the helmet. First drill a 3/32-inch (2.38 mm) hole through one side of the helmet and into the bird's head. Plug the hole with a 1-inch (2.5 cm) length of the round reed that sticks out a bit like a horn on the helmet. Repeat the process for the other side.

The Rare Spotted Luffa-Footed Orange-Beaked Carolina Shorebird is a cousin to the Gourdrunner. It's also made out of an ornamental gourd, but has feet made out of luffa gourds and its top knot and tail are gourd vine tendrils.

Making the Springtail

22. To create the springs for the springtail, cut lengths of copper wire in sizes appropriate to the bird's body. Coil each length around a pencil, leaving a 2-inch (5 cm) length of straight wire at the end of each spring.

23. Use the awl to pierce a hole where the tail will be inserted.

24. Wrap all the straight ends around one another to make one big end. Insert the end into the hole, creating the tail with spiraling tips. Glue in place.

25. Make a spring and add it to the top of the helmet.

Attaching the Wings

26. With the awl, pierce a hole through the wings and body near the top tip of the wings. Apply the glue. Then attach each wing with a copper nail through the hole.

Making the Beak

27. Carefully cut open the stem beak with the utility knife and gently spread the two pieces apart with your fingers. Bend down close and you can probably hear the happy chirp of the Gourdrunner: "Gourd-Day, Gourd-Day!"

VACATION CLOCK

Although this clock functions, it doesn't really work. With nonsensical numbers, the clock is always on vacation! Looking at it reminds you how wonderful it is to just relax and be in time—instead of rushing to be on time. You'll have a gourd time dyeing, burning, and carving the clock, so enjoy every minute!

Materials

Canteen gourd, cleaned

1 stick in a length proportionate to the clock face

1 tiny ornamental gourd

4 tube-shaped beads cut from a dipper gourd (or beads of your choice)

Flat black enamel spray paint

Leather dye: British tan, light brown, black

Vacation Clock goat template, page 122

Transfer paper

Transparent tape

Clear satin lacquer spray finish

Standard quartz clock movement with AA battery (can be purchased at a craft store)

18-gauge (1.00 mm) wire, 3 feet (.91 m) long

Tools and Supplies

Small power saw or handsaw (see page 15)

Pyrography tool with straight-line burning tip

Carving tool with round ball bur (see page 24)

Power drill with ³⁄₃₂-inch (2.38 mm) drill bit, and another bit the size of the clock handshaft

Hair dryer

100-grit sandpaper

Pencil

Paper towels

Cotton swabs

1-inch (2.5 cm) foam brush

Cutting and Decorating the Clock Face

1. Use the bowl-cut technique on page 16 to cut the gourd in half so that the stem is in the center of one of the halves. Use this half, but remove the stem.

2. Clean, sand, and paint the back of the clock with the flat black enamel spray paint.

3. With the pencil, draw a line from 12 o'clock to 6 o'clock on the front of the clock.

4. With the straight-line burning tip, burn over the pencil line.

5. With the foam brushes, dye one side of the clock British tan, and dye the other side light brown.

6. While the British tan side is still damp, dip a cotton swab in black dye (blot off any excess on the paper towel) and make three black dots on the clock face starting just below the area where the stem was.

7. Enlarge the Vacation Clock goat template on page 122. The goat should be in proportion to the size of the clock face. (I love goats because I used to own a goat dairy, but you can use any animal that inspires you to kick up your heels and run free.)

8. Using the tape to hold the transfer paper on the gourd, transfer the pattern onto the clock face.

9. Burn over the pattern line of the goat and color it in with black dye using a cotton swab or small paintbrush.

10. Burn in the numbers on the clock. As you can see from the photo, the hours on the clock don't make any sense, that's why it's named the "vacation" clock.

11. Spray on a coat of clear satin lacquer finish and let it dry.

12. With the round ball bur, carve the dots on the back half of the goat.

Attaching the Clock Movement and the Wire Hanger

13. Locate where you would like to place the clock hands and drill a hole large enough to insert the clock's handshaft. Insert the handshaft of the clock's movement through the drilled hole and secure it with the included mounting nut. Slip on the hour and minute hands and install the battery.

14. Dye the stick with black dye. In the top of the clock, drill two ³⁄₃₂-inch (2.38 mm) holes from which to hang the stick. Insert the 18-gauge wire through both holes. Secure the stick to the top of the gourd.

15. Embellish the hanging wire with tube-shaped gourd beads (cut from a dipper handle and dyed), or your choice of beads and one tiny ornamental gourd.

16. Wrap the remaining wire around a pencil so the wire resembles a spring. After you finish this project, what should you do? Take a vacation!

Dream Village

Like my dream place to live, this whimsical town abides by simple rules: Just Have Fun! Paint your buildings in zany colors, and then populate them with the cheerful little Village People. Keep all the lines distinct by burning the lines deeply with your straight-line burning tip.

Materials for the Gourd Village

Gourd, any size or shape that will facilitate a lid, cleaned

Flat black enamel spray paint

Leather dyes: many assorted colors of your choice

Clear satin lacquer spray finish

Materials for the Village People

Various lengths of gourd tubes for the bodies, cut from the handle of a small-handle dipper gourd or a spoon gourd

Flat gourd scraps, cleaned

Small twigs for neck and legs

Grapevine, small diameter, about 3 to 4 inches (7.6 to 10.2 cm) in length

Leather dye: assortment of colors, including light brown

Quick-set epoxy glue

Clear satin lacquer spray finish

Beads of various colors

Tools and Supplies for Village and People

Small precision jigsaw or handsaw (see page 15)

Pyrography tool with straight-line burning tip

Hair dryer

Power drill with bits appropriate to the size of the grapevine arms

100-grit sandpaper

Pencil

1-inch (2.5 cm) foam brushes

Pliers

Round rasp

Cutting the Gourd and Drawing the Lines

1. Use the lidded-top cutting technique described on page 17 to cut the lid.

2. Clean, sand, and spray the inside of the gourd with the black paint. Let it dry.

3. Just as you would with any village, start this one from the ground up. With the pencil, draw the ground onto the bottom portion of the gourd, giving it a cheerful, uneven appearance.

4. Draw in the various storefronts and start building your houses. Try not to make too many straight lines. The windows aren't square, the doors aren't straight. There's an abundance of chimneys, a tree here and there, church steeples at the top. Don't worry about perspective—it doesn't matter in dream places.

Burning in the Lines

5. Use the straight-line burning tip to burn over your pencil lines. Make sure all of the burn lines connect to each other and are deep enough to create reservoirs to hold the dyes.

Coloring the Design

6. Use the foam brushes and leather dyes to color the village in happy and bright colors of your choice. Dry sections with the hair dryer.

7. Protect your finished piece by spraying a light coat of clear satin lacquer spray finish. Let it dry.

43

6. Spray a light coat of satin lacquer spray finish to the heads. Dry thoroughly.

7. Use the rasp to file a groove in the back of the bottom portion of the head where you'll attach the twig neck. Glue the back of the head onto the neck and let it dry.

8. Glue the beads onto the face to resemble the eyes and mouth. Let them dry. Lift the lid off the gourd village, then drop in a figure for each secret wish. It's fun and it can't hurt. And who knows—it might work!

Making the Village People

1. Cut the bodies of the people in various lengths from the handles of the dipper gourd or spoon gourd. With the foam brush, dye them light brown. Dry thoroughly with the hair dryer.

2. Cut the twigs for the legs, finishing them with an angle at the foot end. Insert the legs into the bodies and secure them in place with glue. Let them dry.

3. Drill armholes on each side of the bodies. The size of the holes will be determined by the diameter of the grapevine arms. Cut the grapevine arms to size, insert them in the holes, and glue in place.

4. Make the necks by inserting twigs into the top of each body. Glue them in place.

5. With the pliers, bend and crimp off random pieces of the gourd scraps to make the heads. Dye the faces with bright-colored dyes and dry them with the hair dryer.

A gourd looks best when you fill almost every space with elements of your design, including the back side.

HEN HOUSE

Everyone will be clucking in admiration when you show off this gourd bowl with its friendly folk art design and "bird's nest" rim. Simple processes of burning, carving, and dyeing make it a decorative treasure.

Materials

Kettle gourd, cleaned

Grapevine wreath (found at craft stores)

Flat black enamel spray paint

Leather dyes: buckskin, black, British tan, mahogany, light brown,

Hen, Rooster, and Chicks templates, page 120

Transfer paper

Transparent tape

Black artificial sinew

Felt-tip pens, green and red

Clear satin lacquer spray finish

Tools and Supplies

Small precision jigsaw or handsaw (see page 15)

Pyrography tool with straight-line burning tip

Carving tool with round ball bur (see page 24)

Power drill with 5/64-inch (1.98 mm) drill bit

Hair dryer

100-grit sandpaper

1-inch (2.5 cm) foam brushes

Paper towels

Pencil

Small artist paintbrush, size 4 flat shader

Scissors

Tapestry needle

Design Tips

Be sure to soak your grapevines until pliable before you try to shape them into the rim. I used pieces from a grapevine wreath since they were already in a circular pattern.

Cutting and Coloring the Gourd

1. Cut the opening of the gourd using the Hills-and-Valleys technique described on page 16. (Save the top portion to use in later steps to practice carving and burning.)

2. Clean, sand, and spray the inside of the gourd with the black paint.

3. Use the foam brush to apply the buckskin dye over the entire surface of the gourd. If the color is too yellow, add a couple of drops of medium brown dye to the buckskin dye and reapply. The brown dye will aid in enhancing the texture of the gourd skin. Wipe off any excess dye with the paper towel.

4. While the dye is still moist, apply medium brown dye to the top 2 inches (5 cm) of the gourd. Using a paper towel, blend the brown dye down and into the buckskin dye. This technique presents a nice shading effect at the top. (See the photo.) Hasten the drying time with a hair dryer.

5. Copy the Hen, Rooster, and Chicks templates on page 120, enlarging them to fit the circumference of your gourd.

Adding the Chicken Design

6. Use the tape to hold the transfer paper to the gourd. With the pencil, trace the hen, rooster, and chicks onto the front of the gourd.

7. Burn in the lines with a straight-line burning tip. Move the burning tip at a slow, but steady, pace. When you reach a tight turn, rotate both the gourd and the burning tip to finish the turn.

8. Draw a horizontal wavy line all the way around the bottom portion of the gourd to simulate the ground. Draw in some mountains. Burn in these lines.

9. Use the small paintbrush and black leather dye to color in the chickens and the rooster. The two chicks are reversed in color (no two chicks are alike, remember!). Paint the middle chick mahogany with a black wing and comb, and the other chick black with a mahogany wing and comb. Color the beaks for both chicks with British tan dye. Let the colors dry thoroughly.

10. To create the dots, use the round ball bur and carve in the dots (see the photo for guidance). Notice that the chicken on the left has both small and large dots. To achieve this effect, press down the carving bur lightly to create small dots, and a little harder for the larger dots. (Use the discarded gourd top to practice making the dots.) The chicken in the middle has clusters of three dots, which gives the design another dimension. Lastly, carve a dot for the eyes.

11. Lightly draw in the tufts of grass, stems, leaves, and a heart shape for the flower.

12. Use the green felt-tip pen to color the grass, stems and leaves. Color the heart-shaped flowers with the red pen.

13. To seal and protect your work, apply a coat of satin lacquer spray finish. Dry thoroughly.

14. To make and attach the grapevine to the gourd rim, follow the instructions for the pine needle rim in the Sycamore Leaves & Pods project on page 62.

15. So the chickens know where to come home to roost, be sure to sign and date your art piece on the bottom!

EGG IN THE NEST

Just like its hatched parents, this egg is polka-dotted and has feathers! The grapevine keeps it warm and cozy.

Materials

Nest egg gourd, cleaned

1 grapevine bird nest (premade at craft stores or you can make it yourself)

3 guinea hen feathers (at craft stores)

Leather dye: black

Clear satin lacquer spray finish

Tools and Supplies

Carving tool with a round ball bur

Hair dryer

Awl

1-inch (2.5 cm) foam brush

Quick-set epoxy glue

Design Tips

Because the nest egg gourd is small and round, you'll need to be cautious when you carve it. Re-read the safety tips in the carving section on page 24.

Making the Egg

1. Gently press the awl into the bottom of the egg gourd as a handle to hold onto while you work. Using the foam brush, color the gourd with the black dye. Dry with the hair dryer.

2. To make the egg shiny, apply two thin coats of satin lacquer spray finish. Dry thoroughly between coats using the hair dryer.

3. Using the round ball bur, carefully carve the dots on the egg.

Making the Nest

4. Position the three guinea hen feathers and the egg in the nest. When you are pleased with the arrangement, glue in place.

CRAYON, COLLAGE & COLOR BOWL

What's so amazing about this graceful bowl is that it has three different decorative techniques, and each is wonderfully easy to accomplish. The simple combination of dye, crayons, and collage materials makes the bowl a marvelous do-together family or school art project.

Materials

Kettle gourd, cleaned

Flat black enamel spray paint

Leather dyes: buckskin, light brown, British tan, black

Black crayon

Tissue paper, several sheets

Acrylic matte medium

Clear satin lacquer spray finish

Tools and Supplies

Small precision jigsaw or handsaw (see page 15)

Hair dryer

100-grit sandpaper

Pencil

1-inch (2.5 cm) foam brushes

Small artist paintbrush, size 4 shader

Cutting and Dyeing the Gourd

1. Use the straight-cut technique described on page 17 to remove the top portion of the gourd.

2. Clean the inside of the gourd. Sand the inside top portion, then spray with the black paint. Let it dry.

3. Using the foam brush, coat the entire outside of the gourd with buckskin leather dye. Dry with the hair dryer.

4. With the pencil, make a mark approximately 2½ inches (6.4 cm) down from the top of the gourd. Draw a line from this point around the entire gourd. Repeat this line approximately 3 inches (7.6 cm) down from the first line. The gourd is now divided into three design sections.

5. Using a foam brush, dye the top portion of the gourd with light brown dye. .

6. While the light brown dye is still damp, use the paintbrush to apply black dye around the rim of the gourd. The black dye should be allowed to run a little, to give an exciting "primitive" look. Then apply the black dye in the same manner to the first pencil line.

7. Dye the bottom third portion of the gourd with one coat of British tan dye. While the dye is still damp,

use the paintbrush and black dye to color over the second pencil line. Again, let the black dye run a little. Dry with the hair dryer.

Designing with Crayons

8. Use the black crayon to draw simple, elementary shapes in the center portion of the gourd. These can be stick people, swirls, squares, steps, circles, dots, etc. Draw over your design again with the black crayon. The waxed crayon acts as a resist and repels the dye.

9. With the hair dryer set at a low temperature, slowly melt the crayon design. Heat the crayon just enough to melt it. If it's too hot, the crayon will run.

10. Dip a foam brush into the light brown dye and color over the crayon shapes. Make sure to leave some light buckskin colored background for contrast. The dye will repel once it comes into contact with the waxed crayon.

Collaging

11. Collage the bottom portion of the gourd with the tissue paper. Follow the same collage technique described in the Asian-Influence Bowl on page 104, using the acrylic matte medium and a foam brush. Tissue paper can be pulled apart into two sections. Apply one layer of tissue for a light color effect or two layers of tissue paper for a darker effect.

12. Coat the tissue paper using a foam brush and light brown dye. Let it dry.

13. Spray a coat of satin lacquer spray finish and let everything dry thoroughly before you move the bowl. Can you make an entire bowl with the crayon technique, instead of just one section? Sure! Crayon away!

Design Tips

Red, green and purple crayons also work. (If this looks child-like, it's supposed to! You're having fun!)

Ladies from the Caves

I'm fascinated by prehistoric paintings found in caves all over the world. Images of generations of women sitting around the fire passing on wisdom to their daughters inspired my design, created with many colors of dye, and basic pyrography and carving techniques. The striking basket reed rim enhances the evocative beauty of the gourd.

Materials

Tall cylinder-shaped gourd with a wide bottom and narrow opening, cleaned

2 pieces of #8 round basket reed, at least 9 inches (22.9 cm) long

Flat black enamel spray paint

Ladies from the Caves templates, page 121

Transfer paper

Transparent tape

Leather dyes: buckskin, light brown, British tan, aqua green, purple, light blue, black

Clear satin lacquer spray finish

Black waxed linen thread, 5 yards (4.57 m) long

Tools and Supplies

Small precision jigsaw or handsaw (see page 15)

Pyrography tool with straight-line burning tip

Hair dryer

Carving tool with a cylinder square cross-cut bur and a round ball bur (see page 24)

Power drill with $^{15}/_{64}$-inch (5.95 mm) drill bit

100-grit sandpaper

Pencil

1-inch (2.5 cm) foam brushes

Cotton swabs

Small artist paintbrush, size 4 flat shader

Scissors

Cutting and Decorating the Gourd

1. Cut the opening of the gourd using the angle-cut technique described on page 17.

2. See the tips on page 18 for cleaning gourds with small openings. Clean, sand, and spray the inside of the gourd with the black paint.

3. Enlarge the templates on page 121, or design your own ladies. Tape the transfer paper to the gourd; with the pencil, trace the cave ladies so they dance all the way around the gourd.

4. Burn in the lines of the patterns with the straight-line burning tip. For lots of decorating ideas, see the longer instructions in the Women of the World project on page 116. Move the burning tip at an even and steady pace. When you reach a tight turn, rotate both the gourd and the burning tip to finish the turn. A lower temperature is also helpful when you're doing this.

5. Mix a few drops of light brown dye into the buckskin dye. Apply this color to the background of the gourd.

6. Dye the top 2 inches (5 cm) of the gourd with medium brown dye. While the brown dye is still damp, use the paintbrush and black dye to paint a ring under the brown section. Let this dye blend together, creating a beautiful shading effect. Add two more rings by burning them in over the black painted ring. Feel free to make the rings in whatever style you want.

7. Use a cotton swab to apply the black dots with leather dye to the brown area at the top.

8. Using the foam brushes and leather dyes, color the cave ladies. Follow the color combinations and design shown in the project in the photo, or make your own.

9. To protect and seal the gourd, spray a coat of clear satin lacquer spray finish over the entire gourd. Dry with the hair dryer.

10. Now it's time to dress up the ladies. Carve in the dot accents using the round ball bur. Use the cylinder square cross-cut bur to create earrings and necklace.

Making the Reed Rim Treatment

11. With a foam brush and black leather dye, dye the round reed pieces and let them dry.

12. Choose a spot on the neck of the gourd that is appropriately placed for the rim. Drill two $^{15}/_{64}$-inch (5.95 mm) holes on opposite sides of the top rim to accept the round reed.

13. Insert the round reed into one hole, allowing it to exit through the gourd and enter the hole on the opposite side. Add the second piece of reed in the same manner. With scissors, cut the ends of the reed at an angle to desired length.

14. Now, you'll wrap the reed with the thread. When you begin wrapping, leave a 3-inch (7.6 cm) tail of the thread hanging loose. (You'll use this tail to tie a knot when you finish the wrapping design.) Holding on to the tail, lay the thread over the reed. Wrap over and under the first piece of the reed then over and under the second piece.

15. Stretch the thread tightly across the neck of the gourd to the reed pieces on the opposite side. Repeat the same wrapping over and under process on these reed pieces. Then tightly stretch the thread across the back of the neck of the gourd to the first reed pieces.

16. Continue wrapping until you have made seven complete wraps. Tie a knot with the tail you left hanging at the start. Leave enough thread at the end to decorate it with beads, if you want. Once you've learned this unique rim treatment, you can use it to add an elegant final touch to almost any other gourd. To enhance the ancient imagery on the gourd, display it surrounded by candles.

Dyan Mai Peterson, *Five Points*, 1996, leather dye, grapevine handle, beads, rim treatment of artificial sinew. Photo by Tim Barnwell

BOWL WITH NATURE WEAVINGS

Making this magnificent bowl is one of the most pleasurable things I do. I really enjoy gathering all the natural materials. Then when I'm weaving the decoration, one beautiful piece at a time, the work is so peaceful it feels like a meditation.

Materials

Basketball gourd, cleaned

Chair weaving cane (size: common 3.5 mm), 8 yards (7.32 m)

Weaving materials:
> Natural materials such as small twigs, vines, dried grasses, cording, hemp, thin strips of bark and pine needles or anything else you want

> Cotton fabric of your choice, about the size of a table napkin

> Coconut fiber (can be purchased at craft stores), 1 yard (.91 m) long

> Cheesecloth, cut into thin strips

3/16-inch (4.7 mm) flat basket reed, 1 yard (.91 m) long

1/4-inch (0.6 mm) flat basket reed, 1 yard (.91 m) long

Leather dyes: assorted colors of your choice, including light brown and black

Felt-tip pens in colors of your choice (optional)

Fabric dye in colors of your choice (optional)

Flat black enamel spray paint

Clear satin lacquer spray finish

20 round flat beads, any size, with any number of holes

Black waxed linen thread

Tools and Supplies

Small precision jigsaw or handsaw (see page 15)

Hair dryer

Power drill with 17/64-inch (6.75 mm) drill bit

100-grit sandpaper

1-inch (2.5 cm) foam brush

Paper towels

Bucket of water

Ruler

Pencil

Scissors

Clothespin

Quick-set epoxy glue

Paper clip (optional)

Making the Gourd Bowl

1. Cut the opening of the gourd using the bowl-cut technique shown on page 16.

2. Clean, sand, and spray the inside of the gourd with the black paint. Let it dry.

3. Use the foam brush to apply light brown dye over the entire outer surface of the bowl. Wipe off any excess dye with a paper towel. Dry thoroughly with the hair dryer.

4. Apply one light coat of satin lacquer spray finish over the entire outer surface of the bowl. Let it dry.

Preparing the Materials for Weaving

5. Soak the weaving cane in the bucket of water for about 20 minutes to make it pliable. If the cane is dry it will crack and break.

6. Pre-soak any plant materials, such as reed, twigs, or grasses for a few minutes in water to keep them pliable while weaving. If you are using a felt-tip pen to color any of the pieces, first wipe off any excess water on the material, then apply the pen.

Making the Framework for the Weaving

7. Now you'll drill holes in the gourd to create the framework for your weavers. With the ruler, measure down about 2 1/2 inches (6.4 cm) from the rim of the gourd. Place a row of pencil marks spaced about 1/2 inches (1.3 cm) apart around the entire gourd. Don't worry about being too precise. These holes will be covered up later by your weaves.

8. Drill a hole at each mark all the way around the bowl.

9. Next you'll lace the cane through the holes. With the scissors, cut the end of the cane at an angle. This will allow the cane to enter into the hole more easily and will prevent the cane from shredding, making the whole process go more quickly.

10. From the outside of the gourd, insert the cane through one of the holes into the inside. Leave a 3-inch (7.6 cm) tail. With the clothespin, clip the tail to the rim of the bowl to help hold the cane in place while you wrap it.

11. Lace the cane in and out of all the holes around the entire bowl. Be careful not to wrap too tightly. Leave the cane loose enough to allow space to insert the weaving materials. When you have returned to the starting point, cut the cane, leaving 1 inch (2.5 cm) at both ends. Overlap the ends and attach them together with quick-set epoxy glue. Secure the glued joint with a clothespin or paper clip while it dries thoroughly.

Weaving the Materials

12. I like to start with the fabric because it's the focal point of my design, but you can start with any weaver you want. Start weaving by inserting the weaver at a diagonal into strips of the cane framework. Weave the piece under and over the cane until you reach the rim. (See figure 1.) How many cane strips you'll weave with depends on the length of your weaver. When you've reached the bowl rim, clip off the end of the weaver, making sure its end is underneath the strip of cane wrapping so it will be secure. Use a touch of glue to keep the end in place.

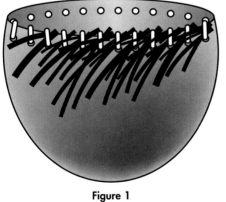

Figure 1
How to insert the weavers under and over the laced cane

13. Continue to weave with your assortment of materials, under and over, and clip all their ends. Sometimes, because the materials have different widths or thicknesses, you won't be able to weave a particular weaver all the way around. That's okay. Simply insert the weaver however possible so that it's secure and tight with its fellow weaver.

14. When you're finished, all the holes will be covered up and you'll have an abundance of weavers placed diagonally, covering the top portion of the gourd. As a final touch, clip the bottom ends at various angles so they look pleasing.

15. Let the woven bowl dry overnight.

Adding the Final Touches

16. The soaked wrapping cane and soaked weaving materials will shrink overnight. You may need to add a few more weavers up under the previous weaving to tighten all the weavers.

17. With the foam brush and black leather dye, color the cane on the inside of the bowl. You may need two or three coats to cover it completely. Dry thoroughly between each application of dye.

18. Add buttons or beads wherever you'd like. Sew them onto weavers with linen thread. Do you have any weaving materials left over? Don't throw them out! Save them for another project.

Design Tips

Collecting and Coloring the Weaving Materials

Take your time collecting and coloring the weaving materials. Collect a combination of textures, sizes, and shapes that will give harmony to the weaving. Choose a range of colors but keep them in the same color palette so they work well together. Start with the fabric. Its colors will be the inspiration for the colors you choose to dye the other weavers. Earth tones complement gourds and work well with the natural materials used in the weaving. I chose an African print because I loved its exotic pattern (in fact, it was a table napkin I found in an import shop) but any earth-tone fabric will work well. How much weaving material you will need to collect depends on the size of your bowl.

I used several different coloring media. For example, I dyed the cheesecloth with British tan leather dye because I had it on hand, but I could have used fabric dye or even a felt-tip pen. To color the reed and other plant materials, you can use fabric dye, leather dye, or felt-tip pens.

CARVED FLOWER VASE

The bas-relief carving technique reveals a gourd's beautiful creamy underskin. No need to add color in the carved area—the contrasting colors and textures of the gourd itself make the stunning design.

Materials

Chinese bottle gourd, or any gourd that has a neck, cleaned

Flat black enamel spray paint

Flower and leaf template on page 122

Transparent tape

Transfer paper

Leather dye: mahogany

Tools and Supplies

Small precision jigsaw or handsaw (see page 15)

Pyrography tool with straight-line carving tip

Carving tool with both a cylinder square cross-cut bur and a round ball bur (see page 24)

100-grit sandpaper

Pencil

1-inch (2.5 cm) foam brushes

Design Tips

Make cutout copies of the flower shapes and space them on the gourd to work out your design before you trace the flowers.

Cutting and Coloring the Gourd

1. Cut the opening of the gourd using the straight-cut technique described on page 17. Save the top to practice your carving in step 7.

2. Clean, sand, and spray the inside of the gourd with the black paint.

3. Use the pencil to draw the curves and dips design on the bottom and top portions of the vase. (See the vase in the photo.) Use the straight-line burning tip to burn over the lines.

4. With a foam brush and mahogany dye, color the gourd from the bottom up to the burn line. Also dye the neck about 3 inches (7.6 cm) down from the rim.

Carving the Design

5. Copy the flower and leaf template on page 122, reducing or enlarging the pattern to fit the proportion of your gourd.

6. Tape the transfer paper on the gourd and with the pencil, trace on several flowers. Space them randomly, leaving room for the stems and leaves. Trace the stem and leaf pattern among the flowers.

7. Practice your carving technique on the portion of the gourd you cut off in step 1 to determine how much pressure you'll need to use on the gourd body. If the skin is soft, carve with light pressure; if the skin is hard and dense, carve with more pressure or raise the speed on your carving tool. For the most attractive bas-relief appearance, try to keep the carved areas at an even depth.

8. Use the round ball bur to carve out the background, removing the top layer of the gourd shell all around the design lines. Use an even pressure for the best results. Be careful, as it is possible to run into a soft spot, which might cause the bur to dig in too deeply. But don't worry. If that happens, use fine-grit sandpaper to smooth out the area. Carve out the entire background, but leave the neck untouched. Continuing to use the round ball bur, carve a dot in the center of each flower.

9. Use the cylinder square cross-cut bur to carve the veins in the flower. Use this same bur to make a tiny dot at the end of each vein.

10. After you've accepted your applause for this project, make another version in reverse, using the incised technique described on page 24. On this one, the flowers will be incised into the hardshell and be cream-colored. The background will be the darker color of the gourd skin.

Design Tips

Unlike other gourd projects, you won't spray this one with a clear finish because spray would darken underskin and eliminate the contrast in color with the outer skin.

Rice Bowl with Chopsticks

Did I paint the wonderful calligraphy marks on the pot with leather dye? Or burn them in, or carve them? No—I drew them with a hot glue gun! Every gourd project presents another opportunity to create a new technique. This one turned out to be terrific.

Materials

Gourd with a shape suitable for a bowl, cleaned

Flat black enamel spray paint

Leather dye: buckskin, light brown, olive green, black

Clear satin lacquer spray finish

2 chopsticks

Black waxed linen thread

Assortment of beads of your choice

Tools and Supplies

Tools and Supplies

Small jigsaw or handsaw (page 15)

Pyrography tool with straight-line burning tip

Hair dryer

Power drill with 5/64-inch (1.98 mm) drill bit

100-grit sandpaper

Pencil

1-inch (2.5 cm) foam brush

Paper towels

Small artist paintbrush, size 4 flat shader

Hot glue gun with glue sticks

Pocketknife

Small round file

Cutting and Coloring the Bowl

1. Cut the opening of the bowl using the straight-cut technique described on page 17. Set the top of the gourd aside as scrap for practicing the gluing technique in step 7.

2. Clean and sand the inside of the gourd. Spray the inside with black flat enamel paint and let it dry.

3. Draw a pencil line approximately 2 to 2½ inches (5.1 to 6.4 cm) down from the rim of the bowl.

I randomly draw lines rather than measure them to create a loose, more artistic look. Burn in the line with the straight-line burning tip.

4. Use the foam brush to apply buckskin dye to the entire bowl. You may need to add a little light brown dye to the buckskin if the color seems too yellow. Wipe off any excess dye with a paper towel.

5. While the buckskin dye is still damp, use the paintbrush and the olive green dye to color the burned line on the lower portion. (To make olive green dye, mix a few drops of medium brown and aqua green dye.) Let the olive green dye run together with the buckskin dye to create a lovely watercolor effect. Dry thoroughly.

Adding the Glue Decoration

6. With the pencil, draw an Asian-inspired design on the top one-third of the gourd. Use your imagination and have fun.

7. (Practice the following method on a scrap piece of gourd first.) Set the bowl on its side and work one section of the design at a time. With the hot glue gun, follow your design lines. Don't worry about the "spider webs" the glue gun creates—they enhance the design.

8. After you have placed hot glue on all of your design lines, use the foam brush to cover the entire top portion of the gourd with light brown dye, covering over the glue lines. You may want to apply two coats for a darker color.

9. While the brown dye is still damp, use the artist paintbrush to paint black dye along the burn line. Again, let it run.

10. Use the hair dryer and slowly dry the brown and black dyes. Be watchful not to let the dryer melt the glue.

11. Let the hot glue cool to room temperature.

12. Next you'll need to remove the glue from the gourd. Warm the glue with the hair dryer one small section at a time. It will be difficult to remove the glue if it's too hot, so keep the dryer at medium heat. With the pocketknife, carefully peel off the glue, revealing the pale design lines beneath.

13. Paint the top edge of the bowl with black dye. Spray with the clear satin lacquer finish.

Adding the Chopsticks and Beads

14. Position the chopsticks on top of the gourd in the center so that the pointed ends of the chopsticks are ¼ inch (0.6 mm) apart, while the opposite ends are about 1 inch (2.5 cm) apart.

15. With the pencil, mark the gourd on each side of both sticks. With the small round file, make a groove on the rim where each end of the chopstick will rest firmly. Place the chopsticks in the grooves.

16. Drill a small hole in the gourd on each side of the chopsticks. Lace black linen thread through the holes, creating an "X" pattern on top of the chopsticks. Tie the ends in a knot, leaving enough thread to tie on beads of your choice. To continue the Asian motif, display the bowl on a mat of bamboo reed or hand-made paper.

Button Bowl & Vases

Buttons add a delightful touch to this vivacious bowl and its two vase companions. Leather dyes blend into one another at their edges to create the lovely watercolor effect.

Materials

Kettle gourd with a smooth surface, cleaned

Flat black enamel spray paint

Leather dyes: aqua green, purple, orange, yellow, oxblood, light blue, olive green

Clear satin spray lacquer finish

Assortment of colored buttons or dyed flat bone beads, with two holes

Black waxed linen thread, 1 yard (.91 m) in length

Assortment of tiny colored beads (optional)

Tools and Supplies

Small precision jigsaw or handsaw (see page 15)

Power drill with 3/32-inch (2.38 mm) drill bit

100-grit sandpaper

Pencil

1-inch (2.5 cm) foam brushes

Design Tips

The dyeing techniques used in this project work best when the surface of the gourd has a smooth skin. If the skin is porous, the dye will sink into the skin and not blend nicely.

Cutting and Coloring the Bowl

1. Cut the gourd open using the bowl-cut technique on page 16. Save the top piece to experiment with color in step 3.

2. Clean, sand, and spray the inside of the gourd with black paint. If you want to place food in the bowl, see the information on food-safe finishes on page 19. Let it dry.

3. Use the foam brushes and leather dyes to cover the gourd with vibrantly colored abstract shapes. Make your own shades by adding a drop or two of another color. Experiment. (To make olive green dye, mix a few drops of medium brown and aqua green dye.)

Test the colors on your scrap piece of gourd. Apply your first color to the bowl.

4. While the first color is still wet, apply a second color, just up to the edge of the first color, but not overlapping it. The colors will merge, giving a wonderful watercolor effect.

5. Continue this method, designing small and large areas of color. This is an abstract design, so you don't have any rules to follow but your own good design sense. Add color anywhere or add any amount of one color.

6. Spray with a coat of clear satin lacquer finish and let it dry.

7. Repeat steps 1 to 6 to make the vases.

Adding the Buttons

8. Using the 3/32-inch (2.38 mm) drill bit, drill two holes into the gourd at each spot where you want to place a button. I used 14 buttons in this bowl, but you can use as many as you wish, depending on the size of your gourd and the variety of your buttons.

9. Lace the black waxed linen thread from the inside of the gourd through to the outside and then through the buttonholes. Knot the thread to secure the button. As a final touch, at the two loose ends of thread, tie a decorative knot or a tiny colored bead.

10. Use the same painting techniques to make matching pieces, such as the two small vases in the photo, or a pair of candlesticks (see the Geometric-Inspired Candlesticks & Vase project on page 72).

Sycamore Leaves & Pods Basket

It takes time to make this stunning basket, but it's actually quite easy. All the designs are created with pens you can buy at your local craft store, so you don't need any carving or pyrography tools. Once you learn the basic techniques for the elegant pine needle rim and the woven handle you can make them for all other kinds of gourd bowls.

Materials for the Bowl

- Kettle gourd, cleaned
- Flat black enamel spray paint
- Leather dyes: buckskin and medium brown
- Sycamore Leaves template, page 121
- Transfer paper
- Transparent tape
- Water-based felt-tip pen, medium green
- Fine-point permanent felt-tip pen, black
- 2 black architectural pens, sizes .05 and .01 (can be purchased at craft stores)
- Clear satin lacquer spray finish
- Extra fine-point liquid gold paint marker

Materials for the Pine Needle Rim

- About 29 long-leaf pine needles (depending on the size of the gourd opening), 10 to 13 inches (25.4 to 33 cm) in length
- Black artificial sinew, about 4 times the length of the opening in the gourd
- Quick-set epoxy glue

Materials for the Wrapped Handle

- "D" basket handle with sharp top, 10 x 14 x ⁷⁄₈ inch, (found through basket suppliers)
- Four long strips of chair weaving cane, size common, 3.5 mm (found through basket suppliers)
- Flat black enamel spray paint
- Leather dye: medium brown
- 4¹⁄₂-inch (12.7 mm) wooden beads with ³⁄₁₆-inch (4.76 mm) hole
- 2³⁄₁₆-inch (4.76 mm) diameter dowel rods, 1¹⁄₂ inches (3.8 cm) long
- Wood glue

Tools and Supplies for the Gourd Bowl

- Small precision jigsaw or handsaw (see page 15)
- Hair dryer
- 100-grit sandpaper
- 1-inch (2.5 cm) foam brushes
- Paper towels
- Pencil
- Small coin

Additional Tools and Supplies for the Rim and Handle

- Power drill with ³⁄₃₂-inch (2.38 mm) bit (to fit the tapestry needle, or awl) and ¹³⁄₆₄-inch (5.16 mm) drill bit (to attach the handle)
- Bucket of water
- Large tapestry needle
- Awl
- Cloth tape measure
- Scissors
- Newspaper
- Rubber gloves
- Spray bottle filled with water

Design Tips

Especially for beginners, it's a smart idea to start applying the pattern on the back of your gourd, so by the time you reach the front, you've perfected your technique. Although I use the same size leaf on my design, you may choose to use three different sized leaves. Depending on the size of your gourd, you'll use six to eight leaf patterns. Consider cutting out the patterns and temporarily spacing them out on the gourd with tape to make sure they all fit before you actually draw them on the gourd.

THE GOURD BOWL
Cutting and Coloring the Gourd

1. Cut the opening of the gourd using the Hills-and-Valleys technique shown on page 16. Save the top portion of the gourd for testing your colors and design techniques.

2. Clean, sand, and spray the inside of the gourd with the black enamel paint.

3. Use the foam brush to apply buckskin leather dye over the entire surface of the gourd. If the color is too yellow, add a couple of drops of medium brown dye to the buckskin dye and reapply. This gives the color an "aged" look.

4. While the dye is still moist, apply medium brown dye to the top 2 inches (5.1 cm) of the gourd. Using a paper towel, blend the brown dye down and into the buckskin dye. This technique presents a nice shading effect at the top. (See the photo on page 63.) Hasten the drying time with the hair dryer, if you wish.

Transferring the Leaf Pattern

5. Copy the Sycamore Leaf template on page 121. You may need to reduce or enlarge the pattern to fit the circumference of your gourd.

6. Use the tape to hold the transfer paper on the gourd; with the pencil trace the sycamore leaf design in a continuous path around the entire top portion of the gourd. Trace lightly over the lines and veins of the leaves to set their design. Leave space around each leaf for the stems and pods. For a more natural effect, vary the space between the leaves, as well as the angle of each leaf.

Coloring the Leaves, Pods, and Stems

7. Using the medium green water-based felt-tip pen, color inside the lines of the leaves.

8. With the black .05 architectural pen, draw the veins onto the leaves.

9. Use the small coin to trace a circle for the pods, placing three pods between each leaf. To give an artistic balance, alter the placement of the pods, as shown in the photograph.

10. Use the black fine-point permanent felt-tip pen to color each pod.

11. Create the spikes on each pod with the black .01 architectural pen.

12. Lightly pencil an arched stem line from every other leaf. Continue this process all the way around the gourd, connecting all the leaves. To complete the design, add leaf stems where needed. There is no right or wrong way to add stems. (I know sycamore leaves don't really have tendrils like gourd vines, but I couldn't resist! If the gourd bug strikes you, too, add tendrils!)

13. Lightly pencil in all the stem lines, connecting the pods to the leaf stems. Use the green pen to color over the pencil lines.

14. Black permanent markers have a tendency to run and can really make you have a bad gourd day. Therefore, spray a light mist of clear satin lacquer finish over the entire gourd to seal the black ink. That means a really really light coat. If you spray a heavy coat, your pods will run all over the gourd! Let the finish dry thoroughly.

15. Apply a second light coat of clear satin lacquer spray finish. Let it dry thoroughly.

16. Use the extra fine-point liquid gold paint marker to add dots on the pods. Don't spray over the gold paint marker.

THE PINE NEEDLE RIM
Preparing the Pine Needles and Piercing the Rim

17. Soak the pine needles in the bucket of water for about 20 minutes or until they are pliable.

18. Use the tape measure and pencil to measure and mark holes about 1/4 inch (6 mm) down from the rim of the gourd bowl and about 1/2 inch (1.3 cm) apart all the way around the rim. Using the drill or the awl, gently (very gently) pierce holes the size of the tapestry needle at the marks.

Stitching the Rim

19. Thread the needle with the black artificial sinew.

20. You'll be doing a simple whipstitch technique to make the rim. Starting at the top of one of the "hills" on the rim, insert the needle and sinew into a hole from the outside of the gourd. Pull the sinew all the way through the hole onto the inside of the gourd, but leave a 4-inch (10.2 cm) tail at the end. Use this tail and the sinew to tie a knot on the inside wall of the gourd. Don't cut off the tail end. You'll need it to tie off your last stitch later.

21. Next, thread the same hole again, pulling the sinew all the way through, but leave enough sinew to make a small loop on the outside.

22. Tuck a small bundle of pine needles into the loop, then pull the sinew taut, holding the pine needles in place on the gourd. Lay the bundle out on the rim. With the stitches on the subsequent holes, you'll stitch over the rest of the pine needle bundle to keep it secure against the rim. Use the appropriate number of pine needles for your gourd. I used nine needles in each bundle for the large-sized gourd in the photo. Also be careful how tightly you pull the sinew. Too tight and you'll crease the pine needles; too loose and they'll look sloppy.

23. Repeat the stitching for each hole. Add a pine needle bundle at a hole that is on top of a "hill." If the bundles get too thick, cut off some pine needles in the middle of the bundle where they won't be seen.

24. When you have stitched all the way around and returned to the starting point, repeat the process, stitching a second time in each hole. Continue to stitch the remaining pine needles onto the gourd until you have run out of pine needles. When you have reached the beginning for the second time, tie a knot with the tail end of the thread you saved in the beginning and add a drop of glue to hold it.

THE WRAPPED CANE HANDLE
Cutting and Painting the Handle

25. When laid down, with sides that slope in and come together in a rounded top, the "D" basket handle resembles the letter "D". The flat bottom of the handle connects the two sides. You'll need to eliminate that flat bottom in order to fit the handle on the gourd. Measure and mark about ½ inch (1.3 cm) up the handle from the base on both sides, and saw off the base.

26. Spray the handle with two coats of flat black enamel spray paint. Allow the paint to dry completely between coats. To save time, also spray the black paint on the four ½-inch (1.3 cm) wooden beads and the two ³⁄₁₆-inch (5 mm) dowel rods that will be used to attach the handle to the gourd.

Wrapping the Handle

27. Choose four of the longest pieces of cane from the coil to wrap the handle. Soak the cane in water for about 20 to 30 minutes. Soaking will make the cane pliable so it won't crack and break while wrapping.

28. Cane has a flat rough side and a smooth rounded side. You'll wrap the handle to show off both sides, creating an exciting look of texture and twist. Here's how: Place the cane smooth side up on the inside of the handle at an angle, at a point 1½ inch (3.8 cm) up from the bottom of the handle. (See fig. 1 on next page.)

29. With your left thumb, hold the cane in place. Wrap around the handle two times to keep the end of the cane in place. (If you're left handed, reverse the instructions.)

30. Wrap the cane around the handle five more times. You now have a total of seven wraps with the smooth side out, which should cover the bottom of the handle. If you need more wraps to cover the bottom, make them. Pull the cane taut. Every wrap should fit snugly against the previous wrap.

The wrap and twist method creates a handle with beautiful texture.

31. Now you'll see both the smooth and the rough sides of the cane in each wrap. Continue wrapping, but each time you wrap the cane around the outside of the handle, hold down cane with your thumb and twist the cane upward to reveal the opposite, or rough, side. After you dye it, this weaving technique results in a fantastic design that alternates between and light and dark. Keep the cane wet by misting it with the spray bottle.

32. Cover the entire handle with the wrap and twist method in step 31. The outside of the handle will be twisted, while the inside will be alternating rough, then smooth.

33. At some point you'll run out of cane, and need to splice on a new wrapper. Presoak the new wrapper.

34. Fold the old piece at a right angle up on the handle out of the way. Add a new wrapper by sliding about 1 inch (2.5 cm) of one end of the new piece underneath the canes already wrapped and then start wrapping it around the handle; as you do, you'll cover the loose end of the first piece and secure it. (See fig. 2.) Continue wrapping until you reach almost to the end of the handle.

35. Stop twisting the cane when you reach a place that is exactly even with the first set of wrapping you did at the very beginning. Duplicate now what you did with the first wrapping, making seven wraps around the handle. Clip off the end of the last cane, leaving a 1-inch (2.5 cm) tail. Then tuck the tail up under the previous wraps, as in diagram 1.

Dyeing the Handle

36. Dye the handle outdoors on newspaper and use rubber gloves. Use a foam brush to coat the cane handle with the medium brown leather dye.

37. While the dye is still wet, submerge the handle in a bucket of water to wash off the excess dye. Set it aside and let it dry. The handle will dry in different shades of light brown, in a wonderful striped aged effect.

Attaching the Handle

38. Mark a center point right below the cane on each side of the handle and drill two $\frac{13}{64}$-inch (5.16 mm) holes. Don't drill through the cane!

39. If you're a beginner, call in your gourd friend because this step can be a two-person job. Place the front of the finished gourd in front of you and determine where the handle is to be located. One person needs to hold the handle in place while the other person is locating the center. This is best done by standing over the top of the gourd and looking down.

40. With the handle in the desired position, insert the awl through the hole in the handle and make a pilot hole in the gourd. Repeat this procedure on the opposite side. Drill the holes through the gourd using the $\frac{13}{64}$-inch (5.16 mm) drill.

41. Place two drops of wood glue into two of the beads and set them aside. Insert the dowel into the handle and through the gourd. Push the dowel into the hole in the bead on the outside of the gourd. Insert a wooden bead onto the dowel on the inside of the gourd. Repeat the process on the opposite side of the gourd. With the handle in place, let the glue dry. Once you've mastered this wrapping technique, you can apply it to all kinds of other shaped handles.

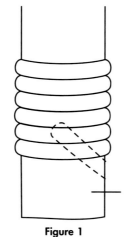

Figure 1
How to start wrapping the handle

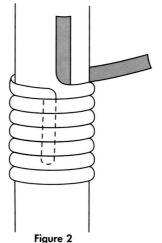

Figure 2
How to splice on a new wrapper

Beautifully Practical

Sistrum, A Musical Gourd

~

Shake yourself out of the doldrums with this V-shaped sistrum, a traditional percussion instrument found all over the world. Just jiggle it and the metal beads roll against one another and rattle gently. The unusual burnished surface is easy to achieve with simple carving and pyrography techniques.

Materials

Dipper gourd, cleaned

Sturdy stick, at least 12 inches (30.5 cm) long

Leather dyes: buckskin, medium brown

Clear satin lacquer spray finish

Quick-set epoxy glue

Beads:
3 large metal beads or metal discs to rattle
2 medium metal beads or discs to rattle
1 cylinder shaped bead as support
Assortment of small decorative beads

Black waxed linen thread

Coconut fiber (found at basket supply stores), hemp, or cotton rope dyed brown, 12 inches (30.5cm) long

Tools and Supplies

Carving tool with both a cylinder square cross-cut bur and a round ball bur (see page 24)

Pyrography tool with straight-line burning tip

Hair dryer

Handsaw (see page 15)

Power drill with 5/64-inch (1.98 cm) drill bit

Pencil

1-inch (2.5 cm) foam brushes

Cotton swabs

Paper towels

Pliers

Making the Sistrum Gourd Body

1. With the pencil, mark a cut line 1 inch (2.5 cm) above the ball on the handle of the gourd. Don't cut off the handle yet. Use it to have something to hold onto while you're decorating the gourd.

2. Use the cylinder square cross-cut bur to carve shapes onto the ball of the sistrum, giving it texture. Carve the entire surface of the gourd, one small section at a time. Carve anything you like: abstract shapes, squiggles, squares, circles, even a secret message to someone.

3. With the foam brush and buckskin dye, color the entire ball. The dye should cover and soak into all of the carved areas.

4. With the brush and medium brown dye, color a 1-inch (2.5 cm) band at the top.

5. Here's how to give the surface an exciting texture: Dip a cotton swab into the medium brown dye, wiping off the excess on a paper towel. Randomly dye some of the carving marks, leaving some of the carvings buckskin-colored. Turn the straight-line burning tip on its side. Using a circular motion, randomly burn over the top of some of the carvings, leaving others untouched. This technique gives it a burnished look.

6. Spray one coat of satin lacquer spray finish. Dry with the hair dryer.

Design Tips

The beads in this project serve several purposes. They are decorative, make the sounds of the instrument, hold the center beads in place, and even support the stick frame. So expand your creativity in the choice of your beads. If you don't have metal beads, use tiny bells, or make discs from tin can lids or rolled copper sheeting from the craft store.

7. With the handsaw, cut off the gourd handle at the cut line. From the handle, cut three sections to make three tube-shaped beads, about 1/2 inch (1.3 cm) long or so to match the size of your gourd. Dye them, let them dry and put them aside for now.

Making the V-Shaped Stick Frame

8. The stick frame holds three sections of beads. The top two bead sections are the noisemakers; the bottom one serves to keep the parts of the stick held apart. You'll measure and drill three holes in the stick before you split it in half to make the V-shape. First measure a point about 2 inches (5.1cm) down from the top of the stick and drill a hole completely through it. Drill another hole 1 1/2 inches (3.8 cm) down from the first hole. Drill the last hole 1 1/2 inches (3.8 cm) down from the second hole. Of course, you'll adjust these measurements if your instrument is substantially larger.

9. Next you want to split the stick into a V-shape. Draw a line 10 inches (25.4 cm) down the center of the stick. With the saw, cut the stick lengthwise along the line. Make sure you don't cut the stick all the way to the end. You need it solid at the end to stabilize it in the gourd.

10. Insert the uncut end of the stick into the gourd. Glue it in place inside the gourd and let dry. Use the foam brush to dye the stick brown. (Tip: The stick will expand from the moisture of the dye, so if you dye it before you glue it in place, it might be too thick to fit.)

11. With the pliers, flatten the metal beads into discs.

12. Gently open the stick with your fingers, just enough to insert the cylinder support bead between the last set of holes that you drilled in step 8. Insert black waxed linen thread into the holes on both sides of the stick, and through the bead to hold it in place. Add beads on both ends and tie knots to hold them. If your bead hole is too large, add a tiny bead and another knot to hold it all together.

13. Repeating the same process, string the two medium size metal beads through the center holes. Then string the larger beads through the top holes.

14. Using the black waxed linen thread, tie around the stick the three tube-shaped beads that you cut from the gourd dipper in step 7. String a bead onto the thread and tie a knot to secure it in place.

15. Add a final decorative touch by wrapping the coconut fiber (or hemp or dyed cotton rope) around the glue joint where the stick enters the gourd and glue in place. Shake the sistrum vigorously to initiate it at full energy. If you still need more energy, make another sistrum and shake them both!

Dyan Mai Peterson, *Hat No. 2*, 1998, carved, pyrography, leather dyes, pine needles, beads, sticks. Photo by Evan Bracken

Dyan Mai Peterson, *Village Festival*, 2001, carved, pyrography, basket reed, hand-made copper beads, glass beads, waxed linen thread. Photo by Evan Bracken

WARM-GLOW LAMPSHADE

Set a mood of relaxation in any room with this glowing gourd lampshade. To create an old-time look, add a "crack" on the shade and then stitch it with artificial sinew. A warm ray of light seeps through the crack.

Materials

- 1 medium gourd in a shape and size suitable for a lampshade
- Small metal lamp with paper lampshade and light bulb (can be purchased at an import, lighting, discount, or craft supply store)
- Leather dye: buckskin, light brown, mahogany, black
- Clear satin spray lacquer finish
- Tapestry needle
- Black artificial sinew
- Black beads (enough to sew one to every other hole in the lacing at the top of the shade)

Tools and Supplies

- Small precision jigsaw or handsaw (see page 15)
- Pyrography tool with straight-line burning tip
- Carving tool with cross-cut bur (see page 24)
- Power drill with ³⁄₃₂-inch (2.38 mm) bit
- Hair dryer
- 100-grit sandpaper
- 1-inch (2.5 cm) foam brushes
- Small artist paintbrush, size 4 flat shader
- Cotton swabs

Making the Lampshade

1. Remove the paper from the store-bought lampshade frame. This will reveal a frame with a hoop and two wire loops that clamp onto the light bulb. Set the frame aside.

2. Cut out the lampshade from the gourd. Use the straight-cut technique (on page 17) for the top and the bowl-cut technique (page 16) for the bottom.

3. Clean and sand the inside of the lampshade.

4. Use the foam brush to coat the inside of the shade with buckskin dye. Allow it to dry.

5. Near the top of the shade, draw three separate pencil lines composed of four arcs. The connecting arcs will form four corners. (See the photo.) It's not necessary to measure the lines exactly. The uneven lines give it a touch of whimsy.

6. Burn in the pencil lines with a straight-line burning tip.

7. Use a foam brush to apply light brown dye to the entire outside of the shade. Carefully dye the top and bottom edges.

8. Use a foam brush to apply the mahogany dye to the middle portion where the carving will be. Allow the dye to run into the light brown dye at the top portion of the shade. Dry with the hair dryer.

9. With the paintbrush, apply black dye between the two sets of arcs. Allow the dye to flow over the bottom burn line. If too much dye flows over, wipe off excess dye with a cotton swab. Dry with the hair dryer.

10. Spray with a coat of clear satin lacquer finish and let it dry.

11. Use the cross-cut bur to carve abstract shapes, circles, lines, squares—any shape that comes to mind. (You may want to practice first on a gourd scrap.)

Adding the Crack and Rim

12. Place the lampshade in front of you and determine where you would like the design crack to be placed. With a pencil, draw the crack onto the gourd.

13. Cut along the crack line with the precision jigsaw or the handsaw. Use caution when cutting this crack. Make sure your hand is not in the way of the saw blade.

14. Drill holes an equal distance apart on both sides of the crack. With the needle and black artificial sinew, lace an "X" design over the crack. Tie a knot in the back to secure in place. (By the way, you can keep yourself in stitches by creating and fixing cracks in all kinds of gourd projects.)

15. About ½ inch (1.3 cm) down from the top of the rim, drill a row with an even number of holes that are about ½ inch (1.3 cm) apart. (I put 18 holes in the lampshade in the photo.)

16. Insert the needle and sinew two times through a hole, back to front, pulling taut each time. Add a black bead to every other hole and secure each with a knot.

17. Continue sewing two stitches in each hole all the way around the gourd. The stitches will form a row of "V"s around the rim. Tie a knot at the end. Turn on the lamp and totally enjoy the warm mood it radiates.

Geometric-Inspired Candlesticks & Vase

I found the inspiration for the design and color palette of these candlesticks and vase from an old pillow made in Pakistan. Geometric motifs from all over the world—American Southwest, Aztec, Greek, Celtic, African, and others—all look wonderful on gourds. Simple carving and pyrography techniques accentuate the clean lines.

Materials

- 2 gourd tops, cleaned
- 2 metal candle cups (can be purchased in craft stores)
- 2 candles, sized to match the holders
- Flat black enamel spray paint
- Leather dyes: buckskin, mahogany, and black
- Clear satin lacquer spray finish

Tools and Supplies

- Small precision jigsaw or handsaw (see page 15)
- Power drill with drill bits to fit your candle cups
- Pyrography tool with straight-line burning tip
- Carving tool with round ball bur (see page 24)
- 100-grit sandpaper
- Round rasp
- Pencil
- 1-inch (2.5 cm) foam brush

Making the Candlesticks

1. Cut off the tops of the two gourds, using the straight-cut technique described on page 17. (Or use scrap gourd tops, if you have them.)

2. Sand the bottom of the gourds to flatten them so they'll rest securely on a tabletop.

3. Clean and sand the insides of the gourd candlesticks. You don't have to paint the insides of the gourds if you don't want to since they won't show. Do paint the candle cups, though, because they look better when painted. Scuff them a bit with the 100-grit sandpaper first so they'll hold the paint better, and spray with the black paint.

4. Drill a starter hole in the top of the gourds and then use the round rasp to carve out a hole for the metal candle cups.

5. With the pencil, draw the geometric shapes on the gourds. Use the candlesticks in the photo as a guide or make up your own design.

6. Using the straight-line burning tip, burn in all the design lines.

7. Using the foam brushes and the leather dyes, color all the shapes. Again, use the photo as a guide or create your own color palette.

8. Spray with clear satin lacquer spray finish.

9. Use the round ball bur and carve in all the dots.

10. If you want to make the companion vase (and why wouldn't you, it looks so marvelous with the candlesticks), use the same design principles. To make the handsome V-shape rim treatment on the vase, see the instructions for the Dotted Horse Utensil Holder project on page 78.

BEADED HANGING BERRY VESSEL

~

The unique wet-on-wet watercolor dyeing technique creates an antique look that makes this gourd vessel seem to be dripping with berries. Fill it with items that are as beautiful and functional as it is, such as artist brushes or carved wooden utensils.

Materials

Kettle gourd, cleaned

24 long-leaf pine needles

Flat black enamel spray paint

Leather dyes: buckskin, medium brown, mahogany, aqua green

Clear satin lacquer spray finish

Gold marker

Brown waxed linen thread

Assortment of beads

Quick-set epoxy glue

Tools and Supplies

Small precision jigsaw or handsaw (page 15)

Hair dryer

Power drill with ³/₃₂-inch (2.38 mm) and ³/₁₆-inch (4.76 mm) drill bits

100-grit sandpaper

Pencil

1-inch (2.5 cm) foam brush

Cotton swabs

Scissors

Cutting and Dyeing the Gourd

1. Use the lidded-top cutting technique described on page 17 to cut off the top of the gourd to make the vessel. (Save the bottom for another project, such as the Sycamore Leaves & Pods Basket project on page 62.)

2. Clean, sand, and spray the inside of the gourd top with the black paint.

3. Use the foam brush to coat the outside of the gourd with the buckskin dye. If the color looks too yellow, add a few drops of the medium brown dye to the buckskin and repaint the gourd.

4. Mix the aqua green dye with a few drops of the medium brown dye to make an olive green dye. While the first coat of buckskin dye is still wet, dip a cotton swab in the olive green dye. Dab the olive green dye at random areas around the top of the rim. Allow the dyes to run together to simulate leaves.

5. While the olive green dye is still damp, dip another cotton swab into the mahogany dye. Make berry clusters on top of the leaves by dabbing clusters of dots over the olive green dye. Dry thoroughly with the hair dryer.

6. To seal the gourd and protect your work, apply a fine mist of clear satin lacquer spray finish and allow it to dry. If you're planning to hang the vessel in an area that has a lot of moisture, such as a kitchen or bathroom, apply two or three more coats, drying the gourd thoroughly between each coat. (Be careful not to use too much lacquer in any one coat, or it will run and create drips.)

7. Use the gold marker to apply clusters of dots on top of the berries.

8. Using the ^{3}/32-inch (2.38 mm) bit, drill holes ^{1}/4 inch (.5 cm) down from the rim and ^{1}/2 inch (1.5 cm) apart all the way around the gourd.

9. Use the waxed linen thread to lace the pine needles through the holes in the rim of the gourd in small bunches, overlapping the needles as you go. See the Pine Needle Rim technique in the Sycamore Leaves & Pods project on page 62.

Adding the Hanging Beads

10. Using the ^{3}/32-inch (2.38 mm) drill bit, drill holes around the perimeter of the gourd, just beneath the pine needle rim. From these holes you'll hang the strands of beads. Make as many, or as few, holes as look good.

11. Make one strand of beads at a time, since you will probably want them to be various lengths. Cut a piece of waxed linen thread, slide on the beads, slip one end through the drilled hole and knot it on the back side. Knot the other end to keep the beads in place. Put a drop of glue on either end. Add two strands of beads to each of the holes. (For a Victorian touch, fill the gourd with potpourri and add a tassel accent at the bottom.)

Adding the Hanger

12. With the ^{3}/16-inch (4.76 mm) bit, drill three holes on one side of the gourd, in the center of each "hill."

13. Cut off three pieces of waxed linen thread and insert the end of each thread into a hole. Tie them securely inside and add a drop of glue to each.

14. Gather the three loose ends of thread and adjust them so that the gourd hangs level. Tie a knot at the top of the threads to secure them in place and add a drop of glue. Save all your gourd tops, such as the ones you might have cut off to make the Hen House project on page 45, to make more vessels.

THIEF POT

~

The lid of the traditional African thief pot fits so precisely, it's said that any thieves who try to steal the treasures in the pot will be caught as they struggle to replace the lid. Placement of the design over the lid rim adds to the illusion that the gourd is uncut. When people discover the bowl has a lid, they invariably break into it—with delighted surprise.

Materials

Gourd with a shape to create a lid, cleaned

Flat black enamel spray paint

Leather dyes: buckskin, light brown, mahogany, black

Thief Pot fish template on page 121

Transparent tape

Transfer paper

Clear satin lacquer spray finish

Tools and Supplies

Small precision jigsaw or handsaw (see page 15)

Pyrography tool with straight-line burning tip

Hair dryer

Carving tool with round ball bur (see page 24)

Pencil

100-grit sandpaper

1-inch (2.5 cm) foam brushes

Paper towels

Small artist paintbrush, size 4 flat shader

Cutting and Coloring the Gourd

1. With the pencil, draw the design of your lid rim on the top portion of the gourd. Using the lidded-top cutting technique described on page 17, cut out the lid.

2. Clean and sand the insides of the gourd bowl and the lid and spray them both with the black spray paint. Note: If you want to put freshly baked cookies or other food items into the pot, see the information on food-safe interior finishes on page 19.

3. Use a foam brush to apply the buckskin leather dye over the entire surface of the gourd and lid. If the color appears to be too yellow, add a couple drops of light brown dye to the buckskin dye and re-apply. The brown dye will enhance the texture of the gourd skin. Wipe off any excess dye with a paper towel.

4. While the dye is still moist, use a foam brush to apply mahogany dye to the top portion of the lid and blend it down and into the buckskin dye with the edge of a paper towel. This technique creates a nice shading effect.

Design Tips

To achieve a perfectly fitting lid, cut the gourd with the saw blade at a 90° angle to the surface.

Adding the Design

5. Copy the Thief Pot Fish template on page 121. Reduce or enlarge it, if needed, so it's in proportion to the size of your gourd.

6. Use tape to hold the transfer paper on the surface of the gourd; with the pencil, trace the fish onto the gourd at different angles, leaving some swimming space around each fish. Using the photograph as a guide, trace some of the fish over the cut line of the lid. This design technique helps obscure the lid of the rim. You really will have to look twice to detect the presence of the lid!

7. Use the straight-line burning tip to burn in all of the outlines of the fish design.

8. With the small paintbrush and black dye, color in all the fish. To keep from smearing the dye, use the hair dryer and dry each fish as you go.

9. Spray the pot and lid with a light coat of clear satin lacquer spray finish. Let it dry.

10. Using the round ball bur, carve the eyes of the fish. To tempt your favorite "thieves," fill the bowl with gold foil-wrapped chocolate coins and silver kisses.

Dotted Horse Utensil Holder

Gourds have always been used as containers. It seems only natural to hold that tradition today, especially in our kitchens where containers can be artistic as well as functional. The V-shaped rim treatment, made with artificial sinew, gives a Southwestern look to the top.

Materials

Tall cylinder-shaped gourd, with a wide, flat bottom, cleaned

Dotted Horse template, page 122

Transparent tape

Transfer paper

Leather dyes: buckskin, light brown, medium brown, British tan, black

Felt-tip pens: turquoise, purple, red, green, orange, olive green

Clear satin lacquer spray finish

Tapestry needle

Black artificial sinew

Quick-set epoxy glue

Tools and Supplies

Small precision jigsaw or handsaw (see page 15)

Pyrography tool with straight-line burning tip

Carving tool with a round ball bur (see page 24)

Power drill with 3/32-inch (2.38 mm) drill bit

100-grit sandpaper

Pencil

1-inch (2.5 cm) foam brushes

Cotton swabs

Paper towels

Small artist paintbrush, size 4 flat shader

Making the Gourd Utensil Holder

1. Cut the gourd using the bowl-cut technique described on page 16.

2. Clean and sand the inside of the gourd. Don't paint the interior black if you're using it to hold kitchen utensils.

3. Enlarge the dotted horse template on page 122 to fit the proportion of your gourd. Or make your own design.

4. Use the pencil and transfer paper to trace the template onto the front of the gourd. Hold the transfer paper onto the gourd with the tape.

5. Use the straight-line burning tip to burn in all of the outlines of the design.

6. Using the gourd in the photograph as a model, or your own design, draw pencil lines on the gourd. Make a square around the horses, allowing the lines at the corners to extend out and some to overlap the tail and back leg of one of the horses. (See the photograph.) Don't forget to draw lines on the sides and back of the gourd.

7. Use the straight-line burning tip to burn in all of the lines in the design.

8. Using the foam brushes and the assortment of leather dyes, color in the horses and the earth-tone rectangular background shapes. Dip a cotton swab into the black dye, wipe off the excess on a paper towel, and place dots on the horse. You'll color the smaller, brightly colored shapes later. Use the gourd in the photograph as a model, or make up your own color palette.

9. Now use felt-tip pens in your choice of colors to fill in the smaller abstract shapes.

10. Seal the gourd with a coat of clear satin lacquer spray finish. If you plan to use the gourd in the kitchen, add another coat as extra protection from accidental water damage.

11. Using the round ball bur, carve the dots on the horse and at any other places you wish on the design.

12. Using the small paintbrush and black dye, go over all the design lines excluding the horses.

Making the Rim Treatment

13. Drill holes about $\frac{1}{2}$ inch (1.3 cm) down from the top of the rim and about $\frac{1}{2}$ inch (1.3 cm) apart. Drill an even number of holes—the exact number will depend on the size of your gourd. I used 18 holes in the gourd in the photograph.

14. Insert the needle and the sinew through a hole and pull taut. Leave a 3-inch (7.6 cm) tail that you'll use to tie off the sinew when you finish stitching.

15. Stitch through the hole again, which forms an attractive "V" shape. Repeat double stitching on every hole all the way around the gourd.

16. With the tail, tie a knot at the end. Add a drop of glue to keep the knot permanent. Fill the holder with beautiful, useful objects such as wooden spoons, brushes, or luffa scrubbers.

LIGHT-BURST LANTERN

Vibrant colors and design simplicity transform an ordinary gourd into a lighting sensation. Instead of a candle, a small electric lamp placed inside the gourd makes the lantern safe. Drill bits create the cut-outs that let the light burst through in different sizes and shapes.

Materials

Kettle gourd, with a bottom large enough to cut a 5-inch (12.7 cm) circle to accept the lamp, cleaned

Upright lamp, sometimes called a can lamp, about 4 inches (10.2 cm) in diameter and 7½ inches (19 cm) tall. (These can be purchased at a lighting or discount store.)

Leather dyes: light brown, red, orange, purple, blue, aqua green, buckskin, mahogany, olive green, black

Light-Burst Lantern template, page 121

Transfer paper

Transparent tape

Flat black enamel spray paint (optional)

Clear satin lacquer spray finish

Tools and Supplies

Small precision jigsaw or handsaw (see page 15)

Power drill with drill bits in the following sizes:
⁵⁄₃₂ **inch (3.97 mm)**
⁷⁄₃₂ **inch (5.56 mm)**
¹⁵⁄₆₄ **inch (5.95 mm)**
⁹⁄₃₂ **inch (7.14 mm)**

Pyrography tool with a straight-line burning tip

Carving tool with a round ball bur (see page 24)

Pencil

Small pencil compass

100-grit sandpaper

1-inch (2.5 cm) foam brushes

Making the Lantern

1. Use the angle-cut technique described on page 17 to cut off the top of the gourd.

2. Use the compass to draw a 5-inch (12.7 cm) diameter circle in the center of the bottom of the gourd to accept the can lamp.

Design Tips

Strictly speaking, a lantern doesn't really have an electric lamp inside it. But don't let that tempt you into using candles in the lantern. The insides of the gourd are too dry to light with a candle. For the same reason, only use the low-wattage bulb recommended by the manufacturer of the can lamp

3. Drill a hole in the center of the bottom, insert the saw blade into the hole to get a starting cut, and then cut along the circle line. Remove the circle and cut a notch at the edge of the hole to accept the lamp cord.

4. Clean, sand, and dye the inside of the gourd with light brown leather dye. Let it dry thoroughly.

5. Copy the Light-Burst Lantern template on page 121 or design your own pattern. Use tape to hold the transfer paper onto the gourd surface; transfer the pattern with the pencil.

6. Use the straight-line burning tip to burn in the lines of the design.

7. Using the variety of drill bits, drill different-shaped holes into the design to let the light come through. With the saw, cut out the straight lines of the design.

8. With the leather dyes and the foam brushes, color in all of the design shapes you transferred in step 5. Use the lamp in the photo as guidance or make up your own color palette to fit the décor of the room where the lantern will be placed.

8. Paint the top rim of the gourd black to give it a sophisticated finishing touch. Use the flat black enamel spray paint or black leather dye.

9. Spray on a coat of satin lacquer spray finish. Let dry thoroughly.

10. Put a bulb with the appropriate wattage into the lamp. (Don't use a high wattage bulb; it could get too hot for the gourd.)

11. Insert the lamp into the gourd, resting it carefully on the bottom. Pull the plug through the notch and plug it in. Wow!

Color Me Happy Necklace & Bracelet

How many times do you see people wearing gourds around their necks? Not enough! That's why this colorful, look-at-me necklace makes such a unique gift. It's doubly wonderful when paired with the gourd bracelet.

Materials

- 1 small dipper gourd handle, cleaned
- 3 nest egg gourds, cleaned
- Hardshell shell gourd scrap, cleaned, 5 x 5 inches (12.7 x 12. 7 cm)
- Newspaper
- Leather dyes: buckskin, light brown, British tan, oxblood, aqua green, purple, mahogany
- Clear satin lacquer spray finish
- 1½ yards (1.37 m) black waxed linen thread
- 25 black beads with white dots
- 20 large black bugle beads
- 2 black tube beads (with holes large enough to fit two strands of waxed linen thread)
- Clear glue

Tools and Supplies

- Power drill with 5/64-inch (1.98 cm) drill bit
- Hacksaw
- Utility knife
- Pliers
- Small jeweler's pliers

Design Tips

"Today's gourd scrap is tomorrow's treasure." That's why experienced gourd artists always keep their gourd scraps. The more you work with gourds, the more uses you'll find for gourd scraps.

Necklace

Cutting and Preparing All the Pieces

1. From the small dipper gourd handle, use the hacksaw to cut 27 tube-shaped beads in various lengths, approximately 3/8 to 1 inch (9.5 mm to 2.5 cm). Use the utility knife to cut three of these tubes in half, lengthwise.

2. Cut three nest egg gourds in half. Use the pliers to break them into small pieces. There are 24 nest egg gourd pieces in this necklace.

3. From the hardshell gourd scrap, break off 10 small chunks of gourd with the pliers.

4. Remove all the dried pulp from the back side of each gourd piece. Clean out the pulp from the inside of the tube beads.

5. Lay out newspaper to protect your work surface from the dye. Hold the gourd pieces with the jeweler's pliers, and dip each gourd piece into the color of leather dye you want for it. Use the colors I suggested or create your own palette. Go goofy! Set all the pieces aside to dry.

6. Hold each gourd piece with the jeweler's pliers and cover with a light coat of clear satin lacquer spray finish. Allow them all to dry thoroughly.

7. Drill a 5/64-inch (1.98 cm) hole in the center of each gourd piece.

Combining the Pieces

8. Lay out the finished pieces in the color combination you want. Tip: Between the black and white dotted beads, contrasting colors look best.

9. String the gourd pieces onto the black linen thread randomly, alternating the gourd pieces with the black dotted beads. (See the photo for guidance.)

10. Adjust the necklace so that there is an equal amount of thread left on both ends. Try it on to make sure it's the right length for you.

11. Add 10 large black bugle beads on each side of the exposed linen threads.

12. To secure the necklace, lay out two black tube beads. Take one end of the thread and string it through both beads. Take the other thread and string it through both beads in the opposite direction.

13. At this point you have two strands of thread going through two beads in opposite directions. Tie both ends in a tight knot close to the bead end. Add a drop of glue to secure the knot. The necklace looks especially fantastic against black, which offers a dramatic background for all the colors.

BRACELET

When people admire this fabulous bracelet, you don't have to reveal how inexpensive it was to make with a gourd scrap. Just smile and keep your fashion secret!

Materials

Gourd scrap cut from the top of a gourd, about 10 to 11 inches (25 to 28 cm) in circumference, for the bracelet

Leather dye: aqua green, British tan, oxblood, buckskin, purple, black

Clear satin lacquer spray finish

Tools and Supplies

Carving tool with a round ball bur (see page 24)

Hacksaw

150-grit sandpaper

Cotton swabs

Cutting and Preparing the Bracelet

1. A gourd bracelet is durable if it's at least $\frac{1}{4}$ inch (0.6 mm) thick and 1 inch (2.5 cm) wide. Use the hacksaw to make a straight cut near the top of the gourd. Inspect the diameter of the opening to check that the gourd will be the proper size to fit over your hand. If so, make the second cut about $1\frac{1}{4}$-inch (3.2 cm) down from the first cut and parallel to it. If not, make another cut further down the gourd until you're able to make a band that will fit.

2. Clean the inside of the bracelet, and sand the inside smooth, very gently, to take the sharpness off the outside edge.

Coloring the Stripes

3. With cotton swabs and leather dyes, color the bracelet. Use the photo to guide you, or make up your own color palette, but do make more black stripes than any other color. Place contrasting colors between the black stripes. Alternate the colors and widths of the stripes.

4. While each colored stripe is still damp, apply the next color so that the stripes gently run into each other, giving the bracelet a pretty watercolor effect.

5. Color the edges and inside of the bracelet with the black leather dye, and allow to dry thoroughly.

6. Spray with one coat of clear satin lacquer finish. Allow to dry.

Carving the Dots

7. Using your carving tool with the round ball bur, carve white dots into the black stripes. Safety reminder: both the carving bur and the gourd surface are round. It's important that you support the bracelet tightly so the bur won't run off the surface. You may want to practice carving dots on a gourd scrap before you start on the bracelet itself. What's next? More bracelets in wild colors? Or beautiful earrings with beads that jangle?

EASTER EGGS & BOWL

The secret to these vibrant Easter eggs is an undercoat of white paint that makes the leather dye colors pop out. Keep the egg decorations bold and simple, or go wild with polka dots and stripes. Make some "cracked" eggs, too.

Materials

Small gourd for the bowl, cleaned

12 nest egg gourds (or enough to fill the bowl), cleaned

Leather dyes: buckskin, oxblood, mahogany, aqua green, purple, light blue, orange, yellow, red

Felt-tip pen, blue

Clear satin lacquer spray finish

Flat white enamel spray paint

Tools and Supplies

Small precision jigsaw or handsaw (see page 15)

Hair dryer

Pyrography tool with straight-line burning tip

Carving tool with round ball bur (see page 24)

Power drill with 5/64-inch (1.98 cm) drill bit

100-grit sandpaper

150-grit sandpaper

1-inch (2.5 cm) foam brushes

Pencil

Awl

Cotton swabs

Utility knife

Making the Bowl

1. Cut the small gourd using the bowl-cut technique described on page 16.

2. Clean the inside of the gourd bowl and sand it with the 100-grit sandpaper. Then gently sand the edges of the bowl with the 150-grit sandpaper.

3. Use the foam brush to dye both the inside and outside of the bowl with buckskin dye. Dry thoroughly with the hair dryer.

4. Using the pencil, make a series of shallow "S" curved lines, separated by dots, all the way around the bowl about 1/2 inch (1.3 cm) down from the rim. Don't worry about measuring or making everything too neat—these should be fluid and loose lines.

5. Use the straight-line burning tip to burn in the curved lines around the entire bowl. Use the round ball bur to carve in the dot marks. Color in the carved dots with a blue felt-tip pen.

6. Spray the finished bowl with a coat of clear satin lacquer spray finish. Let it dry thoroughly.

Decorating the Eggs

7. Drill a tiny hole into the flat end of one of the nest egg gourds. Insert the awl into this hole—now the awl is a handle to hold the egg.

8. While you are holding onto the awl handle, spray the nest egg gourd with the flat white enamel spray paint. The underlayer of white paint seals the gourd skin and reveals the leather dyes in pop-out vibrant hues. Most nest egg gourds require two coats of paint. Dry between coats with the hair dryer. When the last coat is dry, set the egg aside.

9. Repeat steps 7 and 8 for the rest of the nest eggs. Warning: Better plan on putting the white undercoat on a lot of eggs, because once you start decorating them with color later, you'll be glad you have many prepared ahead of time!

10. Use a cotton swab and your choice of colors to dye the eggs. All the bright colors complement each other, so there's no such thing as a wrong color combination. Hey, these are Easter eggs—let your imagination hop all over the place!

11. *To create stripes* on an egg, apply a color to the surface. While the dye is still wet, apply a second color, making sure to apply the dye up to the edge of the previous color so they merge together. Repeat this method, using several different colors of dye on one egg.

12. *To make a plaid egg*, use the same technique as in step 11, just make the stripes criss-cross one another.

13. *To make a polka dot egg*, use a cotton swab to coat the egg with red dye. The red dye changes to pink when it's applied to the white-painted egg. Dip a cotton swab into blue dye and apply dots to the egg. Let the dots run. Apply another blue dot on top of the first dot to create a beautiful effect.

14. *To make a "broken" egg,* draw a zigzag line around the circumference of the nest egg gourd with a pencil. With the utility knife, cut along the lines until you've cut through completely and the egg is "cracked" into two pieces. Nest egg gourds usually have thin skins, so cut gently, avoiding excessive pressure. Dye the egg to your liking.

15. Protect the eggs with a coat of clear satin lacquer spray finish. Unlike chicken eggs, which are fragile, whole nest egg gourds are sturdy—so you can hide them anywhere and not worry about little egg-hunters breaking them. And unlike Easter eggs, which have to be eaten or discarded in a few weeks, the gourd eggs can be passed down as family heirlooms from one generation to another. They'll last indefinitely.

Dyan Mai Peterson, *Egg Fit for a Queen*, 2000, hot glue, leather dyes, gold leaf. Photo by Evan Bracken

Dyan Mai Peterson, *Royal Eggs*, 2000, collage of gold and copper leaf. Photo by Evan Bracken

Perfectly Simple Soap Dish

Bring simple luxury to your bathroom with this oh-so-easy gourd soap dish, decorated with a bamboo stick and thread stitching. Add home-made luffa soap to make it extra special.

Materials

Canteen gourd, cleaned

2 gourd scraps, thinner than the canteen gourd, about 2½ x 3 inches (6.4 x 7.6 cm)

Leather dye: medium brown

Bamboo stick (can be purchased in the floral section in craft stores) or any small stick, long enough to overlap the radius of the gourd by 1½ inches (3.8 cm) on each side

Black or brown waxed linen thread

Quick-set epoxy glue

Tools and Supplies

Small precision jigsaw or handsaw (see page 15)

Hair dryer

Power drill with ³⁄32-inch (2.38 mm) drill bit

100-grit sandpaper

1-inch (2.5 cm) foam brush

Paper towels

Pencil

Small round rasp

If you have to, you can cut the needed gourd scraps out of the top portion of the gourd after you cut it in step 1. But I hate to waste a canteen gourd that can be put to better use, such as to make another soap dish at the same time. So try to use up some of your scrap pieces from another gourd.

Making the Soap Dish

1. Using the bowl-cut technique described on page 16, cut the canteen gourd into the shape of a shallow bowl (or as my friend says, into the shape of a Viking ship).

2. Clean and sand the inside of the gourd and the two gourd scraps. Use the sandpaper to sand smooth all the edges, both on the soap dish and the scraps. Then sand flat the bottom edge of the dish so it will rest securely on a countertop or bathtub edge.

3. Using the foam brush, dye the gourd and the scraps with the medium brown dye. Dry with the hair dryer.

4. The bamboo stick will rest in grooves cut into the two scrap pieces. Pencil mark the center of the top edge of the two scrap pieces. Use the round rasp to file out grooves around this point, wide enough to hold the stick.

5. The scrap sidepieces will be sewn onto the soap dish. Here's how. Do one side at a time. Hold the scrap piece in place against the soap dish and drill four ³/₃₂-inch (2.38 mm) holes, all the way through the scrap and into the soap dish. Place the first two holes about ³/₈ inch (9.5 mm) from the bottom and the other two holes about ³/₈ inch (9.5 mm) above them. Use the black or brown waxed linen thread to sew the scrap onto the soap dish using an "X" stitch, connecting all four holes. Secure with a knot inside the dish. Add a tiny drop of quick-dry epoxy glue to hold the knot in place. Repeat for the scrap on the other side.

6. Drill two holes in each scrap piece about ¼ inch (6 mm) below the grooves at the top.

7. Cut the stick, leaving about 1½ inches (3.8 cm) overhang. For a finished touch, cut the ends at an angle. Set the stick in the grooves. Thread through the holes and sew the stick in place, making a nice "X" stitch or some other neat look on top of it.

8. Add handmade luffa soap and a small round luffa scrubber to create a lovely gift package.

Recipe for Luffa Soap

What You Need

Glycerine soap (available at craft stores)

Microwave or double boiler

Microwave-safe container

Chunks or slices of luffa gourd, dried

Soap mold

Raffia to tie a bow

1. Place the desired amount of glycerine soap in a microwave-safe dish. Heat the soap in the microwave for 30 seconds on high, then at 10-second intervals until it's melted. (You can also melt it in a double boiler.) Add fragrance if you wish.

2. Pour the melted soap into the soap mold. Cut up chunks or slices of luffa and insert them into the soap. Let everything cool overnight.

3. Using your thumbs, apply gentle and constant pressure to release the soap from the mold. Tie on raffia for decoration. When the soap melts away, it leaves the wonderful luffa exposed and then you have a great mini-scrubber.

THREE GOURD LOVER GIFT CARDS

You don't need an official occasion to share your love of gourds with your favorite people. Any excuse will do. These gourd gift cards are too large to fit in a normal envelope, so for mailing, wrap them in a pretty package. Better yet, hand deliver them.

GOURD BLOSSOM COLLAGE AND SEED POUCH

Tailor-made for friends with green thumbs, this card preserves the fragile beauty of gourd blossoms. With the seed pouch and simple planting instructions, include a promise to personally help with the harvest.

Materials for the Collage Card

- 1 pressed and dried gourd blossom (or flower of your choice)
- 1 pressed leaf
- 1 gourd tendril or 12 inches (30.5 cm) of 24-gauge (.50 mm) wire
- Blank notecard (140 lb. watercolor) with matching envelope
- Water-soluble felt-tip pen, green
- Acrylic matte medium
- Cream and olive green-colored paper for background
- Olive green ribbon, 30 inches (76.2 cm) long

Materials for the Seed Pouch

- Ornamental gourd seeds
- Small piece of cream-colored cloth netting, 2 x 4 inches (5.1 x 10.2 cm)
- Cream-colored thread

Tools and Supplies for Both

- Scissors
- Cotton swabs
- 1-inch (2.5 cm) foam brush
- Small container of water
- Paper towels
- Sewing needle

Making the Card

1. With your fingers, gently tear the opening edge of the notecard from top to bottom to create an attractive torn edge.

2. Color the torn edge of the card with the green felt-tip pen. Dip a cotton swab in water. Blot off the excess water on a paper towel. Apply the cotton swab to the green inked edge of the card, which will give the edge a watercolor effect.

3. With the foam bush, apply acrylic matte medium to the backs of the cream and green background papers. Layer the papers on the card and press them firmly to attach them. Allow them to dry.

4. Using the foam brush, apply acrylic matte medium to the back sides of the blossom, the tendril, and the leaf. Press the leaf onto the paper, then press the blossom, and finally the tendril. Allow everything to dry.

5. Tie the ribbon onto the card and finish with a bow.

Making the Seed Pouch

6. Fold the cloth netting in half. With the needle and thread, sew around the edges of the pouch, leaving a small opening. Fill the pouch with the ornamental gourd seeds. Sew the opening closed, leaving enough thread for a handle.

GOURD PEOPLE PIN WITH GIFT CARD

Make a whole box of these Gourd People pins, tissue wrap them carefully, and keep them handy as last-minute gifts to attach to gift cards. Human people just love them!

Materials

2 gourd scraps for practicing drawing

#3 round basket reed, about 12 inches (30.5 cm) long, or 4 small twigs (for legs, arms, and neck)

Blank notecard (140 lb. watercolor) with matching envelope

Black and blue textured paper (for background)

Acrylic matte medium

Leather dye: black

Clear satin lacquer spray finish

3 small tendrils of your choice, such as gourd or grapevine, or 3 pieces of 24-gauge (.50 mm) wire, about 6 inches (15.2 cm) long

Black waxed linen thread, about 12 inches (30.5 cm) long

Quick-set epoxy glue

Small colored beads of your choice

Pin clasp

Tools and Supplies

Burning tool with straight-line burning tip

Hair dryer

1-inch (2.5 cm) foam brush

Pencil

Pliers

Scissors

⅛-inch (0.3 cm) fine-tooth rasp

Awl

Making the Gourd Pin

1. Tear the edges of the black and blue background paper. With the foam bush, apply acrylic matte medium to the backs of the paper, then place them on the note card. (See the photo for guidance.) Press them firmly to attach them. Allow them to dry.

2. On one of the gourd scraps, use the pencil to draw an abstract shape resembling a person's torso. This person can have any shape you want: round, square, rectangle, triangle, or any combination. That's the fun of making people pins—everybody looks good!

3. Use the pliers to break the gourd away from the pencil line. If it doesn't break away just where you want it, that's okay. This is an "anything works" pin.

4. Repeat steps 2 and 3 to make the head.

5. With the pencil, draw lines on the body—again, any shapes you want—and burn them in with the straight-line burning tip.

6. Color in the shapes with black leather dye and the foam brush. Dry with the hair dryer.

7. Spray a light coat of the clear satin lacquer finish over everything and let it dry.

8. Make the wire tendrils for the hair by wrapping the wire around one of the basket reeds. Put them aside for now.

9. With the scissors, cut the #3 basket reed (or twigs) for the neck, arms, and legs to the correct length and proportion to the body. Cut the ends at an angle for a finished look. Dye with black leather dye. Dry thoroughly with a hair dryer.

ORNAMENTAL GOURD CARD WITH SEED POUCH

Brighten a friend's rainy day with this special card that promises sunny days ahead. Sign it "Warm Regourds."

Materials

Ornamental bottle gourd (not cleaned)

Blank notecard (140 lb. watercolor) with matching envelope

2 tendrils or 9 inches (22.9 cm) of 24-gauge (.50 mm) wire

Small twig cut to length as a "stem" for the gourd

Rust-colored felt-tip pen

Natural-colored raffia, 1 yard (.91 m) long

2 pieces of textured cream colored background paper

Acrylic matte medium

Quick-set epoxy glue

Tools and Supplies

Handsaw

⅛-inch (0.3 cm) fine-tooth rasp

Scissors

Making the Card and Seed Pouch

1. Follow steps 1, 2, and 3 in the Gourd Blossom Collage and Seed Pouch project on page 91, but use the paper and pen colors for this card.

2. Cut the ornamental gourd in half. Clean out the backside of the gourd.

3. With the rasp, file a notch in the center top of the gourd so it will lie flat on the card when you have added the twig stem. Insert the twig into the gourd and glue it in place. Then place the gourd on the card, glue it in place, and allow it to dry.

4. To make a wire tendril, wrap a piece of the wire around the pencil so the wire resembles a tendril. Glue the wire to the card.

5. Tie the raffia to the inside fold of the card and tie a knot. Add a raffia twist to the top of the gourd.

6. If you wish, add a seed pouch. Just gather the materials and follow the seed pouch instructions in step 6 on page 91.

10. On the back side of the gourd pin, use the round rasp to file the grooves needed in which to lay the neck, arms, and legs. The grooves will allow the pin to lay flat on the card. Glue the gourd pieces in place.

11. Glue on the beads for the eyes and mouth and the wire tendrils for the hair. Let everything dry.

12. String beads of your choice on the black waxed linen thread and tie them to the arms.

13. Glue the clasp on the back of the pin and let it dry.

Making the Gift Card

14. Mark points for two holes on the front of the card where you'll attach the pin. With the awl, pierce two holes.

15. Cut a 6-inch (15.2 cm) length of black linen thread. Insert one end of the thread through the top hole and catch the back of the pin clasp. Insert the other end of the thread into the other hole and tie a bow. When you make all these presents for your friends, make sure to put your name on at least one of them.

CANTEEN HANDBAG

For this jaunty canteen handbag, it was an easy journey from gourd patch to high-fashion gift accessory. The hinges are simple cut-and-sew leather pieces; the handle is silk cord. With its striking design and compact size, the handbag is perfect to carry on any occasion—especially for Saturday night dancing.

Materials

Canteen gourd, cleaned

Flat black enamel spray paint

Canteen Handbag template on page 120

Masking tape

Transfer paper

Leather dyes: buckskin, light brown, medium brown, mahogany, British tan, aqua green, red, black

Felt-tip pens, olive green and purple

Clear satin lacquer spray finish

Leather strips for the hinge and clasp, sized appropriately

Waxed linen thread, black or brown, to match the colors of the handbag

1 yard (91.4 cm) black satin cord

4-inch (10.2 cm) strip of hook and loop tape

Quick-set epoxy glue

1 black bead

7 colored beads

Tools and Supplies

Small precision jigsaw or handsaw (see page 15)

Pyrography tool with straight-line burning tip

Carving tool with round ball bur (see page 24)

Power drill with 5/64-inch (1.98 mm) and 9/32-inch (7.14 mm) drill bits

100-grit sandpaper

1-inch (2.5 cm) foam brushes

Pencil

Scissors

Awl (optional)

Cotton swabs

Cutting and Decorating the Handbag

1. Cut off the top portion of the gourd, using the straight-cut technique described on page 17.

2. Clean, sand, and spray the inside of the two gourd pieces with the black enamel paint. Let them dry. The inside will look quite dramatic when the handbag is opened up.

3. Enlarge the Canteen Handbag template on page 12000 to cover the fronts of the handbag and the lid. Temporarily attach the handbag and the lid pieces with the masking tape. Use more tape to hold down the transfer paper while you trace the pattern onto the gourd pieces with the pencil.

4. Burn the pattern design onto the gourd with the straight-line burning tip.

5. Color in the design using the brushes with the leather dyes, and the felt-tip pens. Follow the color palette shown in the photograph or create your own. Have fun! All the colors look fantastic together.

6. To add black dots, dip a cotton swab in black dye and apply it gently to the gourd surface.

7. To add colored dots, carve dots with the round ball bur wherever you want them and color them in with felt-tip pens.

8. Seal the handbag pieces with the clear satin lacquer spray finish and let them dry.

Making and Attaching the Back Hinge

9. Use the scissors to cut a piece of leather that is long and wide enough to be a serviceable hinge. Fold it in half to create a crease along its width, where it will bend when the handbag is opened.

10. Unfold the leather so it is flat. Measure and mark four points on both the top and bottom halves. Using the awl or the drill with the 5/64-inch (1.98 mm) drill bit, pierce eight holes through the leather.

11. Place the hinge in a vertical position so it will hold the handbag lid to the body. With a pencil, transfer the hole positions in the hinge onto the gourd, and drill the holes into the gourd.

Above the mark left by the blossom of the gourd, the leather hinge holds the two pieces of the handbag together.

12. Attach the hinge to the gourd by sewing an "X" pattern through the holes on the leather and the gourd pieces. Use the waxed linen thread and secure with a knot on the inside.

Making and Attaching the Handle

13. On both sides of the body portion of the handbag, mark points about 1/2 inch (1.3 cm) down from the rim where you'll drill holes for the handbag handle. Drill the holes with the 9/32-inch (7.14 mm) drill bit.

14. Insert the ends of the black satin cord into the holes; secure one end of the cord with a knot. Adjust the cord to your desired length. Then knot the other side.

Making the Leather Front Closure

15. Refer to the photograph to help you design and cut a leather closure for the front of the handbag. Dye it black and let it dry.

16. With the awl, pierce four holes in the top section of the closure. Then, using the waxed linen thread, sew the closure onto the gourd in an "X" pattern. Tie a knot on the inside of the gourd to secure the closure in place.

17. Cut out two circles or squares of the hook and loop tape. Glue one piece of the tape on the leather closure. Glue the other piece on the outside of the handbag at a point where it will meet the piece on the closure.

18. To make a knob for the closure, sew the black bead onto the front bottom of the closure. Add the colored beads for decoration—add a lot more beads to create a sensation.

Dyan Mai Peterson, *Dragonfly Handbag*, 2000, leather dye, felt-tip pens, cotton cord strap, bead fastener. Photo by Evan Bracken

HARVEST TABLE BASKET

~

Display the abundance of your harvest holiday table with this generously sized basket, rimmed with richly colored pine needles. Fill it with hot-from-the-oven biscuits. Or let it overflow with fresh fruit, such as red apples, green pears, and purple grapes.

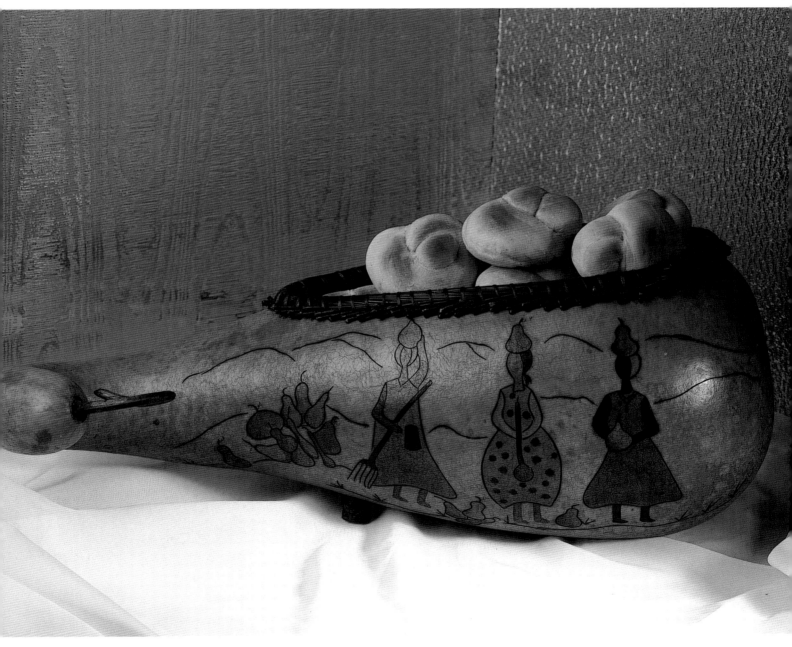

Materials for the Basket and Rim

Gourd with a shape suitable for a basket, cleaned

Section cut from a dipper gourd handle (to create feet, if needed)

2 ounces (56 grams) of long-leaf pine needles

Flat black enamel spray paint

Harvest Basket templates, page 122

Transfer paper

Transparent tape

Leather dyes: buckskin, light brown, medium brown, British tan, black

Clear satin lacquer spray finish

Quick-set epoxy glue (optional)

Plum-colored fabric dye to color the pine needles

Black artificial sinew

Tools and Supplies for the Basket and Rim

Small precision jigsaw or handsaw (see page 15)

Pyrography tool with straight-line burning tip

Hair dryer

Power drill with ⅛-inch (3.18 cm) drill bit

100-grit sandpaper

Pencil

Cotton swabs

Paper towels

1-inch (2.5 cm) foam brushes

Tapestry needle

Cutting and Coloring the Basket

1. Cut the opening of the gourd using the bowl-cut technique described on page 16.

2. Clean and sand the inside. I chose to spray the inside with black paint, as I do for most of my projects, to give it a nice background contrast to the outside colors. And then I use a linen napkin to line the inside when I put food in it. You can do what I did, or follow the instructions on page 19 for food-safe finishes.

3. Copy the Harvest Table Basket templates on page 122. You may need to reduce or enlarge the template so that the design it is proportionate to the size of your gourd.

4. With the tape securing the transfer paper, trace the pattern onto the gourd. Pencil in the mountains and the ground.

5. Use the straight-line burning tip to burn in all the outlines of the design.

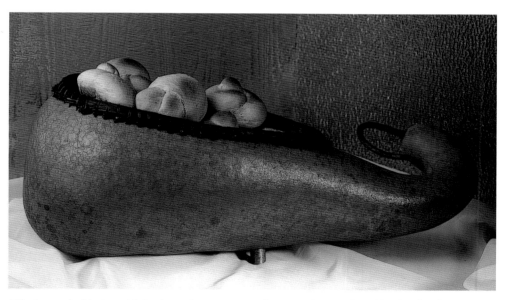

What's wonderful about this basket is that no matter where people sit at the table, they'll still see a beautiful gourd.

6. With the foam brush, apply buckskin dye to the entire outside of the gourd, covering all the burned-in lines.

7. Using a cotton swab, color the harvest ladies' dresses. (Left to right I used light brown, British tan, and medium brown, but do make your own color decisions.)

8. Dip a cotton swab onto black dye and wipe off the excess dye with a paper towel. Place black dots on the dress to resemble polka dots. Dry with the hair dryer.

9. Dye the remaining areas, using the color palette shown in the photograph or make your own color choices.

10. To protect and seal the gourd, spray it with a coat of clear satin lacquer spray finish over the entire gourd. Let it dry.

11. If you need to level the bottom of the gourd, create feet on which to rest it. Here's how: From the handle of a dipper gourd, cut out two ring "feet." Sand the edges of the rings, if necessary, so the bowl rests flat on them. Glue the feet in place.

Design Tips

I love Thanksgiving designs that show people harvesting together, but you can use any design that is appropriate for a large gourd. Consider templates from other projects such as the Sycamore Leaves & Pods Basket (page 62), the Thief Pot, (page 76) or the Hen House (page 45). I've even made some baskets with abstract designs such as those in the Canteen Handbag (page 94) and the Light-Burst Lantern (page 80), and they look fantastic, too.

Making the Pine Needle Rim

12. Use fabric dye to color the pine needles a dark plum color. Follow the manufacturer's instructions on the dye package. The longer you leave the pine needles in the dye bath, the darker the color will be. Rinse the pine needles thoroughly.

13. Using the drill, the tapestry needle, and the black artificial sinew attach the pine needles to the rim. Follow the instructions for the pine needle rim in the Sycamore Leaves & Pods Basket on page 62. But instead of adding a bundle of pine needles at each "hill" on the rim, in this project, which has a flat rim, you'll add two pine needles at each hole as you lace. If the pine needles seem to get too thick in spots, just angle cut them off from the back as you go along. The unadorned backside of the basket has a different kind of beauty— so don't be afraid to allow it to show.

Jana White, *Teapot*, 2000, pyrography, caulking adhesive, acrylic paint. Photo by Evan Bracken

CHRISTMAS STOCKING

It's all made from gourds: the Santa-size plaid stocking, the gilded cuff, the gingerbread man, the star, even the candy cane. Since dried gourds can last indefinitely, this beautiful decoration will become a family heirloom to be enjoyed for generations of happy holidays.

Materials

Hardshell gourd suitable for the size stocking you want, cleaned

Dipper gourd handle, curved like a candy cane, cleaned

Templates for the stocking, its cuff, the star and the gingerbread man on page 120

Transparent tape

Transfer paper

Flat black enamel spray paint

Leather dye: aqua green, light brown, purple, mahogany, light blue

Clear satin lacquer spray finish

Gold shoe polish

Narrow satin ribbon in turquoise, purple and burgundy

5 small gold bells

Quick-set epoxy glue

Extra-fine-point liquid gold paint pen

6 small beads for the gingerbread man, 3 black and 3 pink

Satin embroidery thread in red and purple

Sheet of black construction paper

2 wooden shishkabob skewers, cut into lengths of 5 and 6 inches (12.7 and 15.2 cm)

Tools and Supplies

Power drill with 3/32-inch (2.38 mm), and 13/64-inch (5.16 mm) bits

Small precision jigsaw or handsaw (see page 15)

Pyrography tool with straight-line burning tip

Hair dryer

Pencil

100-grit sandpaper

Scissors

1-inch (2.5 cm) foam brushes

Cutting the Pieces

1. Enlarge all the templates on page 120, so they fit on your gourd.

2. Use the tape to hold the transfer paper onto the gourd; with the pencil, trace the shape of the stocking onto the curved contours of your gourd.

3. Drill a hole in the gourd outside of the pattern line to create a starting point for your cutting. Insert the saw blade into the hole, and cut along the pattern line.

4. Repeat steps 2 and 3 to cut out the stocking cuff, the gingerbread man, and the star from the remaining gourd.

Decorating the Stocking

5. Clean, sand, and spray the back sides of the cuff and the stocking with the black paint. You'll dye the gingerbread man and the star later.

6. With the pencil, draw the heel and toe shapes onto the stocking. Use the straight-line burning tip to burn over these lines. Outline the toe and the heel with little straight lines to resemble stitches.

7. Using the foam brush and the aqua green leather dye, dye the heel and the toe. Dye the rest of the stocking with an array of Christmas colors. Use the purple, mahogany and light blue as I did, use your own color palette. Dry with the hair dryer.

8. Make the stocking look plaid, or quilted, by burning in diagonal lines with the straight-line burning tip.

9. Spray with a coat of the satin lacquer spray finish.

Decorating the Cuff

10. Color the stocking cuff with the gold shoe polish. Let it dry.

11. Drill five evenly spaced holes about ¼ inch (0.6 cm) from the bottom edge of the cuff, using the ³⁄₃₂-inch (2.38 mm) drill bit.

12. Insert the ribbons into the holes and tie a knot in the back of the cuff. Tie the bells onto the ribbons.

13. Glue the cuff on the stocking and set them both aside to dry.

Decorating the Gingerbread Man

14. Use the foam brush to dye the front and back of the gingerbread man light brown. Dry with the hair dryer. Using the gold pen, make squiggled lines to create the "frosting" cuffs on his arms and legs. Glue on the beads to make his black "raisin" eyes and mouth, and his pink vest buttons.

Decorating the Star

15. Dye the front and back of the star with purple dye. Dry with the hair dryer. Use the gold pen to edge the star with small dots.

Making the Candy Cane

16. Use the handsaw to cut the dipper handle into the shape of a candy cane. (A gourd with a round shape would have been formed by the gourd growing along the ground instead of hanging. See the section on shaping gourds on the vine on page 11.) Wrap the candy cane with red embroidery thread to create stripes. To keep the threads in place, glue them wherever needed.

Stuffing the Stocking

17. Create a braid from which to hang your stocking. Drill a ¹³⁄₆₄-inch (5.16 mm) hole in the top left corner of the stocking. Braid a strand of purple embroidery thread to your desired length. Place the braid through the hole and tie a knot to cover it. Secure the other ends of the braid with a knot. Be as creative as you want with the braid.

18. Glue the skewers onto the backs of the gingerbread man and the star. Set them aside to dry.

19. Position and glue the candy cane, the gingerbread man, and the star to the back of the stocking. They're heavy so you'll need an ample amount of the quick-set epoxy glue. (Don't use hot glue, it doesn't last.) Let everything dry.

20. To make the back of the gourd neat and tidy, measure and cut to fit the piece of black paper, and glue it onto the back of the stocking. If you wrap the stocking carefully in tissue paper and store it in a box, it can last for many years.

Dyan Mai Peterson, *Deck the Gourds with Boughs of Holly*, 2001, pyrography, green felt-tip pen, French wire ribbon. Photo by Evan Bracken

Dyan Mai Peterson, *Have a Gourd Holiday*, 1997, carved, leather dyes, reed, ribbon, bells. Photo by Evan Bracken

Ronna Wuttke, *Father Christmas*, 1999, pyrography with washed acrylic. Photo by Evan Bracken

Gale Trujillo, *replica of late 19th century Santa*, 2000, tea-stained paper, wire.
Photo by Evan Bracken

Dyan Mai Peterson, *Angels Among Us*, 2000, holiday wrapping paper, gold leaf, French wire ribbon.
Photo by Evan Bracken

Left: Dyan Mai Peterson and members of the North Carolina Gourd Patch Society, *Celebrating a Gourd Christmas*, Festival of Trees 2001 at Biltmore Square Mall, Asheville, NC, sponsored by the Mountain Area Hospice Foundation.
Photo by Tim Barnwell

simply Fantastic

ASIAN INFLUENCE COLLAGE

I combined two of my loves, collage and Asian art, to design this distinctive bowl. Underneath a thread "net," touches of gold leaf make the bowl sparkle mysteriously—what ancient treasure is held by the delicate web?

Materials

Tobacco box gourd, cleaned

Pressed, dried leaves

Leaf skeletons (can be found outdoors on the ground or purchased from a craft supply store)

Flat black enamel spray paint

Collection of papers including some or all of these:
Hand-marbled paper
Textured paper of any thickness
Papyrus paper
Gift wrapping or tissue paper

Pressed, dried leaves

Leaf skeletons (can be found outdoors on the ground or purchased from a craft supply store)

2 sheets of gold leaf

Acrylic matte medium

Black waxed linen thread

Flat black enamel spray paint

Clear satin lacquer spray finish

Black waxed linen thread

Tools and Supplies

Small precision jigsaw or handsaw (see page 15)

1-inch (2.5 cm) foam brush

100-grit sandpaper

Scissors

Left: **Dyan Mai Peterson**, *Chow Mein*, 1999, chopsticks, leather dye, collage with assorted papers, coins, brass nails, and thread. Right: *Collage No. 32*, 1999, pyrography, carved, leather dyes, assorted papers, beads, coins, wire, reed, waxed linen thread. Photo by Evan Bracken

Design Tips

A gourd bowl collage is an exciting way to experiment with new materials, such as textured hand-made papers from your local art supply store. Personalize your own art piece by using collage materials that have special meaning for you, such as postcards, love letters, poems, and travel mementos.

Cutting and Collaging the Gourd

1. Cut the opening in the gourd, using the straight-cut technique described on page 17.

2. Clean, sand, and spray the inside of the gourd with the black paint. Let it dry.

3. Tear the papers you have chosen for your collage composition and the sheets of gold leaf into small pieces of different shapes and sizes.

4. Use the foam brush to coat a portion of the gourd surface with acrylic matte medium.

5. Begin overlapping and layering the collage components into place on the portion of the gourd covered with the acrylic matte medium. Papers, leaves, leaf skeletons, and gold leaf should be positioned in a random and diagonal fashion.

6. Continue steps 4 and 5 until you've covered the entire gourd. Let everything dry.

7. Spray the finished piece with clear spray lacquer to seal and protect it.

Adding the Thread Netting

8. Use the black waxed linen thread to wrap the entire gourd in a random fashion to look as if it had been captured in a net. To keep the net in place, tie knots where the threads intersect, letting the tails of the knot hang down artistically. At the end of each thread tie a decorative knot.

9. To balance the knotted intersections, add threaded knots in the empty spaces where needed. Warning: Take it from me—collaging on gourds becomes so much fun that you'll you'll probably start a new hobby collecting collage materials everywhere you go.

THREE GOURD SHADOW BOXES

A shadow box, especially when protected with glass, is a simple and elegant way to display gourd art. Premade boxes, complete with pretty matte boards, can be found at craft stores. Repetition is the key to creating dramatic impact in these three shadow box projects.

DIPPER HANDLE SHADOW BOX

The number of dipper handles you'll use in your project will depend on the diameter of the handles and the size of your shadow box. In the shadow box in the photo, there are 14 sections: dipper gourd handles, a bamboo pole, and two bundles of sticks (one bundle is bamboo and the other is honeysuckle vines).

Materials

10 gourd dipper handles of various diameters, cleaned

2 bundles of sticks of your choice, for sections #8 and #12. (I used honeysuckle vine and bamboo.)

1 piece of bamboo (if not available, add one more length of dipper handle)

Shadow box with matte board, 10 x 16 inches (25.4 cm x 40.6 cm)

Leather dyes: black, British tan, mahogany, aqua green, light blue, buckskin, light brown, red, purple

Felt-tip pen, olive green

Black embroidery thread

Quick-set epoxy glue

Clear satin lacquer spray finish

Tools and Supplies

Handsaw

Pyrography tool with straight-line burning tip

Carving tool with square cross-cut bur and round ball burl (see page 24)

Hair dryer

1-inch (2.5 cm) foam brushes

Cotton swabs

Paper towels

Pencil

Small artist paintbrushes, size 4 flat shader

Glass cleaner

Design Tips

In your enthusiasm to have so many coloring possibilities at one time, don't forget to let the dye dry after each application! When you've finished the decoration of each gourd handle, spray it with the clear satin lacquer finish and set it aside. Decorate the dipper handles and combine them in any sequence you desire. Follow the directions below if you want to emulate the sequence in the photograph.

Cutting All the Pieces

1. Using the handsaw, cut the bamboo and sticks and all the dipper gourd handles to fit the width of the shadow box except one. You'll cut the last piece in section #3.

Decorating Each Section

2. Decorate the sections as follows:

Section #1
With the foam brush, dye the gourd handle black. With the cross-cut bur, carve a crosshatch design in a random fashion. (Section #14 is the same, so you might want to make both of them at the same time.)

Section #2
For this gourd handle, dye the whole gourd with British tan dye. Then dip a cotton swab into mahogany dye (wiping off the excess with a paper towel) and place dots in a random fashion. Use the size 4 paint brush and black dye to create random rectangles.

Section #3
Cut this gourd handle a little shorter than the others, leaving room to insert a piece from a smaller-diameter handle in a telescoping manner. Dye the longer piece aqua green and the shorter piece light blue. Paint in black rectangles and carve abstract lines and dots into them with the cross-cut-bur. Insert the light blue length in the aqua green length and adjust them to fit.

Section #4
If you don't have bamboo, dye a length of gourd with the buckskin dye. If you wish, use the straight-line burning tip to emulate the notch on a bamboo pole.

Section #5
Dye the gourd handle with the buckskin leather dye and let dry. Make all the stripes go lengthwise on the handle. Make some with the olive green felt-tip pen, others with British tan dye and a cotton swab, and use the straight-line burning tip to burn in very narrow stripes.

Section #6
Dye the gourd handle black and let it dry. Then carve in round dots with the round-ball bur.

Section #7
Dye the gourd handle light brown and let dry. Use a cotton swab and mahogany leather dye to make two wide stripes. Burn in wavy lines over the stripes.

Section #8
This section is a bundle of bamboo sticks. Tie the bundles with black embroidery thread in two places.

Section #9
Dye the dipper handle with buckskin dye. Use a cotton swab and mahogany dye to create random spirals around it. To add more dimension, burn over the dyed section with the straight-line burning tip.

Section #10
Dye about three fourths of the dipper handle with the red dye and the remainder with purple dye. Add short black dye lines into the red section. To add more texture, burn a line into the black dyed line.

Section #11
Dye the handle black. Carve rectangles and dots.

Section #12
Make a bundle of sticks and tie the bundle together with the embroidery thread.

Section #13
Dye the last dipper handle with buckskin dye. Use a cotton swab and place mahogany dots in a random fashion. Then top each dot with a tinier dot of black dye.

Section #14
Repeat the same procedure for the section #1 handle.

Finishing the Display

3. If you haven't already done so, seal and protect each dipper handle with the clear satin spray finish.

4. If some of the dipper handles don't fit snugly into the shadow box frame, add a drop of glue to secure them in place. (Don't forget to sign and date the matte board before closing up the back of the shadow box.)

5. Clean the glass and insert it into the shadow box.

Nest Egg Gourd Shadow Box

Displayed under glass, an arrangement of vibrantly decorated nest egg gourds becomes a treasured collectible, worthy of hanging on a wall for all to see.

Materials

9 nest egg gourds, cleaned

Shadow box with matte board, 11 x 13 inches (27.9 cm x 33 cm)

Leather dyes: black, British tan, mahogany, aqua green, light blue, buckskin, light brown, red, purple

Felt-tip pen, olive green

Quick-set epoxy glue

Tools and Supplies

Pyrography tool with straight-line burning tip

Carving tool with square cross-cut bur and round ball burl (see page 24)

Hair dryer

Small artist paint-brushes, size 4 flat shader

1-inch (2.5 cm) foam brushes

Cotton swabs

Paper towels

Pencil

Glass cleaner

Making the Shadow Box

1. Use the same methods described in the Dipper Handle Shadow Box project on the previous page, creating a different design for each of the nine nest egg gourds.

2. Space the nest egg gourds in two rows in the shadow box. Remember balance and proportion when spacing them.

3. Mark the final position of each gourd with the pencil and glue them in place.

4. Clean the glass and insert it into the shadow box.

ORNAMENTAL GOURD SHADOW BOX

An array of the amazing variety of shapes and sizes of ornamental gourds becomes quite a conversation piece—so be ready to point out the names of the gourds. People are always curious.

Materials and Supplies

Assortment of ornamental gourds, enough to completely fill the box

Shadow box with matte board, 11 x 13 inches (27.9 cm x 33 cm)

Glass cleaner

Making the Shadow Box

1. Completely fill the shadow box with a variety of shapes, sizes, and types of ornamental gourds that will fit the depth of the shadow box. For contrast in texture, leave some gourds uncleaned.

2. Arrange and adjust the gourds to achieve your desired effect and glue them in place.

3. After cleaning the glass, put it back in the shadow box.

Design Tips

Since ornamental gourds are so easy to grow, consider creating art pieces right in the garden. Wrap wire around the gourds, and as they grow the wire will become embedded in the outer skin. The result is a sculpted, one-of-a-kind ornamental gourd. (For more information on how to shape growing gourds, see page 11.)

MASKED VASE

This eye-catching mask and vase combination is so elegant, it turns any display area into an art gallery. Construction involves only two gourds and several simple techniques: transferring a pattern, dyeing, pyrography, and bead stringing. Sticks placed at an angle on the sides add a surge of power to the piece.

Materials

Gourd with a shape suitable for the mask, cleaned

Gourd that is suitably shaped and sized as a vase on which to attach the mask, cleaned

3 sticks, about the width of a pencil, about 12 inches (30.5 cm) long

Flat black enamel spray paint

Leather dyes: buckskin, light brown, black

Plum-colored fabric dye

Cotton rope, $1/8$-inch (0.3 cm) wide, 3 yards (2.7 m) long

Masked Vase template, page 121

Transparent tape

Transfer paper

Black waxed linen thread

Clear satin lacquer spray finish

Assortment of beads of your choice

2 copper nails

1 flat copper rivet

Quick-set epoxy glue

Tools and Supplies

Small precision jigsaw or handsaw (see page 15)

Power drill with $13/64$-inch (5.16 mm) and $11/64$-inch (4.37 mm) drill bits

Pyrography tool with straight-line burning tip

Hair dryer

100-grit sandpaper

1-inch (2.5 cm) foam brushes

Paper towels

Pencil

Cotton swabs

Awl

Making the Vase

1. Cut the opening of the vase using the angle-cut technique described on page 17.

2. Clean, sand, and spray the inside of the gourd with the black enamel paint. Let it dry thoroughly.

3. Use the foam brush to apply the buckskin dye over the entire gourd surface.

4. While the buckskin dye is still moist, apply light brown dye to the top 2 inches (5.1 cm) of the gourd edge. Using the paper towels, blend the light brown dye down and into the buckskin dye to create a lovely shading effect. Dry thoroughly with the hair dryer. Set the vase aside.

Making the Mask

5. Dye the cotton rope with the plum-colored fabric dye, following the manufacturer's instructions on the package. Submerge the rope in the dye for approximately two minutes. Rinse off the excess dye and set the rope aside to dry.

6. Enlarge the Masked Vase template (on page 110) to fit your gourd. Use the pencil and transfer paper to trace the pattern onto the curved contours of the gourd, holding the paper steady by taping it to the gourd surface.

7. Drill a hole in the gourd just outside the pattern line to give yourself a starting point for cutting. Insert the saw blade of the cutting tool you are using in the hole and then cut out all the lines on the mask shape.

8. Clean and sand the back side of the mask.

9. Using the straight-line burning tip, burn in all design lines on the mask.

10. Use the foam brush to apply buckskin dye to the entire surface of the mask.

11. While the buckskin dye is still damp, dip a cotton swab into the light brown dye and place a dot of dye in the center of every other shape on the forehead of the mask. Repeat using black dye. Let the dyes run, creating a watercolor illusion.

12. With the black dye, color in the eyebrows, eyes, and mouth.

13. Dye the nose and around the eyes light brown.

14. With the straight-line burning tip, burn a ¼ inch (6 mm) dotted line along the edge of the mask, with the dots about ¼ inch (6 mm) apart.

15. Seal the mask with a coat of clear satin lacquer spray finish and dry it with the hair dryer.

Adding the Rope and Beads

16. Next you'll drill holes in the mask so you can hang it on the vase. Work on one side of the mask at a time, starting on the right side. Drill three ¹³⁄₆₄-inch (5.16 cm) holes: one in the top right corner of the forehead, another in the bottom right corner of the forehead, and the third in the middle section of the forehead. Repeat on the left side of the mask.

17. Thread the plum-colored cotton rope through the hole in the top right corner of the mask. Tie a knot on the back side of the mask to secure it in place. Cut off the excess rope. Tie another knot on the front side to cover the drilled hole. Cut the rope to your desired length. Untwist the rope up to the knot to create a fringe-like effect.

18. To create the diagonal thrust for the sticks, you'll make another set of holes on both sides of the mask. With the awl, pierce two small vertical holes to the right side edge of the mask next to the right eye. Pierce two more vertical holes on the other side of the mask, higher up, on the left center of the forehead.

19. Slip the thread into one set of holes and tie on the three sticks. Repeat on the other side. The sticks should now be tied on at a diagonal angle, creating a dynamic design element.

20. Tie beads onto the rope strands you untwisted in step 17 to create a headdress effect.

Attaching the Mask to the Vase

21. Next you'll secure the mask to the gourd vase. With the awl, gently pierce a hole in the center of the eye; to guarantee a tight fit, the hole should be smaller than the copper nail. Repeat on the other eye.

22. Position the mask in place on the gourd vase. Push the nails into the vase, just hard enough to make an indention in the vase. Use the awl to open the holes a bit, and then push the nails into the holes for a tight fit.

23. Pull the mask and the nails out of the vase. Apply a generous amount of quick-set epoxy glue into the holes in the gourd vase and around the nails. Insert the nails back into the gourd vase and let them dry overnight.

24. To create the illusion the mask is hanging from the vase, make the last embellishment. Drill a ¹¹⁄₆₄-inch (4.37 cm) hole about ¾ inch (1.9 cm) down from the rim of the vase. Insert the copper rivet.

25. Tie a piece of the thread to the corner of the mask, loop it around the rivet and secure it to the other corner of the mask. If you wish, fill the vase with tall straight or curly sticks of your choice and place it anywhere it can be easily seen and admired.

Design Tips

The beauty of this mask is the balance between the four elements of pattern, color, texture, and embellishment. Experiment with all four elements on each of your projects to create your own designs.

Gourd-Hearted Mother & Children

I am enthralled with all the different sizes, shapes, colors, personalities, and attitudes that people have. Instead of drawing them on paper, I create three-dimensional images of people with gourds. Like me, once you start making gourd families, you'll be looking for "body parts" every time you visit a farmer's market or gourd show.

Materials for the Gourd Bodies

Whole gourd in a suitable shape for a body, cleaned

Section of a cylinder-shaped gourd for the torso, cleaned

Section of an ornamental bottle gourd for the neck, cleaned

Whole ornamental gourd, round at one end with a short handle, for the head, cleaned

2 ring sections cut from a dipper gourd handle for the earrings, cleaned

1 section of the curved handle of a dipper gourd for the headdress, cleaned

#8 round basket reed for the arms and headdress, 12 inches (30.5 cm) long

#3 round basket reed for the earrings, 6 inches 15.2 cm) long

Leather dyes: black, purple, aqua green, light brown, buckskin, mahogany, olive green

Clear satin lacquer spray finish

Quick-set epoxy glue

Materials for the Headdress

Small twigs

Pine needles

Dried grasses

18-gauge (1.00 mm) wire, about 24 inches (61 cm) long

Tools and Supplies

Small precision jigsaw or handsaw (see page 15)

Power drill with:

17/64-inch (6.75 mm) drill bit for arms, eyes, and headdress

9/32-inch (7.14 mm) drill bit for mouth

3/32-inch (2.38 mm) drill bit for earrings

Pyrography tool with straight-line burning tip

Hair dryer

Carving tool with a round ball bur (see page 24)

100-grit sandpaper

Pencil

1-inch (2.5 cm) foam brushes

Small artist paintbrushes, size 4 flat shader and size 2 liner

Scissors

Cotton swabs

Paper towels

Awl

Cutting All the Pieces

1. From the whole gourd, use the straight-cut technique (page 17) to cut off the top portion to make the body.

2. From the cylinder-shaped gourd scrap, cut out the torso.

3. From the ornamental bottle gourd, cut out the center concave section for the neck.

4. From the dipper gourd, cut off the two earrings.

5. From the dipper gourd handle, cut out a section for the headdress that will be in correct proportion to the size of the mother's head.

6. Sand smooth any of the sharp edges.

Dyeing the Reed Pieces

7. Dye all the reed pieces with black leather dye and let them dry.

Making and Decorating the Body

8. With the pencil, draw the dress design onto the gourd body. Use the photograph as a guide, or create your own design.

9. With the straight-line burning tip, outline the dress design on the gourd.

10. Dye the dress using dyes in purple, aqua green, light brown, buckskin, and mahogany, as shown in the photograph. Or create your own color palette—and don't be timid.

11. While all of the dyes are still damp, dip the small, size 2 artist paintbrush into the black leather dye and paint over the burned-in lines. Dry thoroughly with the hair dryer.

12. Spray with the clear satin lacquer finish. When it's dry, carve in the dots design, using the round ball bur.

Making and Attaching the Torso and Arms

13. Dye the torso piece olive green (or color of your choice). To make olive green, mix a few drops of light brown dye into the aqua green dye. Spray it with the clear finish.

14. Drill two armholes at suitable spots on the torso. Insert the size 8 round reed into the holes and use the scissors to cut the reed to the desired length for the arms, making an angle cut at the ends. Position the torso with the arms onto the body, glue it on, and let it dry thoroughly.

Making the Neck

15. Dye the neck black and let it dry. Spray it with clear finish and let it dry. Using the round ball bur, carve the dots onto the neck. Glue the neck portion onto the torso and let it dry.

Making the Head

16. On the ornamental gourd head, pencil mark the position of the eyes and mouth. Use the $^{17}/_{64}$-inch (6.75 mm) drill bit to make the eyes. Use the $^9/_{32}$-inch (7.14 mm) drill bit for the mouth opening. Dye the head light brown. While the dye is still damp, use the flat shader paintbrush to paint the hair with black leather dye. Make light downward strokes to represent wisps of hair.

17. Now color the eyes and mouth. Dip a cotton swab into the mahogany dye. Wipe the excess onto a paper towel. Insert the cotton swab into the holes of the eyes and mouth, allowing the dye to spread around the openings. Spray the head with the clear finish and let it dry.

Making and Attaching the Earrings

18. Dye the earrings two different colors. (This gal loves to be noticed!) I made one black and one olive green. Let them dry.

19. Drill a hole $^3/_{32}$ inch (2.38 mm) in the center on the right side of the head. Drill a second hole $^1/_4$ inch (0.6 mm) above the first hole.

20. Cut the size 3 round reed in half to create two 3-inch (7.6 cm) lengths. Insert the reed into the bottom hole. Place an earring onto the reed and insert the remaining end into the top hole. Leave enough reed to create a loop. (See the photograph.) Repeat for the other side.

Making the Headdress

21. Dye the headdress section black and let it dry. Spray with the clear finish and let it dry. With the round ball carving bur, carve in the dots.

22. Use the awl to make an indentation on the head where you'll drill the hole to place the headdress. Drill $^{17}/_{64}$ inch (6.75 mm) holes through the center of the headdress and into the head.

23. Cut a 4-inch (10.2 cm) length of the #8 reed and insert it into the holes through the headdress and into the head. Glue it in place.

24. Decorate the head-dress, one side at a time. Make wire spirals with the 18-gauge (1.00 mm) wire and bundle them with the small twigs, pine needles, and dried grasses. Glue them in place.

25. To create the two children, use the same techniques, just use smaller gourds and gourd body parts. If your smaller figures are teenagers, give them a rebellious touch with unique gourd shapes and wild hairdos.

If you color the mother in earth tones, use the same dyes for her children.

WOMEN OF THE WORLD GOURD

Inspired by my love of African art, this gourd captures the universal spirit of all women: each figure is different in shape and size and color, yet they are all united and standing together. Repetition of the design is what makes it so dynamic.

Materials

- **Large whole gourd, any shape, cleaned**
- **Scrap pieces of gourd, similar in thickness to the whole gourd**
- **Women of the World template on page 120**
- **Transfer paper**
- **Transparent tape**
- **Leather dyes: mahogany, British tan, purple, buckskin, aqua green, oxblood, light blue, black**
- **Clear satin lacquer spray finish**

Tools and Supplies

- **Pyrography tool with straight-line burning tip**
- **Carving tool with cylinder square cross-cut but and a round ball bur (see page 24)**
- **Hair dryer**
- **Pencil**
- **6 1-inch (2.5 cm) foam brushes**
- **Small artist paintbrush, size 4 flat shader**

Transferring Templates and Adding Color

1. Copy the template on page 120. Depending on the size and shape of the gourd, you may need to reduce or enlarge the pattern, or shorten or lengthen it to fit. (That's what makes the project so exciting: it's always different. I've made hundreds of these gourds and each one is unique.)

2. Use the tape to hold the transfer paper on the gourd, and with the pencil, trace the rectangles of the bodies all the way around the gourd. Or if you want, use the pattern as a guide and draw them freehand in pencil. Use the straight-line burning tip to burn in all the bodies.

3. Trace or draw each of the ladies' heads. Each head can be a different shape or size. Remember to

Design Tips

This design may look challenging, but when you break it down into sections, it becomes easy. The body of each lady is simple—a rectangle that is narrow at the top and wider at the bottom. Create a combination of ladies whose bodies are thin or wide. Whatever their size, however, all the shoulders of the ladies should be level with each other.

leave enough space between the heads where you will later carve the earrings. (A lady can never be without her earrings!) Burn in the outline of the ladies' heads with a straight-line burning tip.

4. Trace or draw all the legs. Again, these can be short, long, or wide. Burn in the outlines of the legs.

5. Follow the dress designs on the gourd in the photograph or draw your own, adding the arms and hands as you go. Go wild with your own style. Make the dresses whatever designs you want.

6. With the straight-line burning tip, burn in the necklaces, pockets, and any other designs on the dresses, as well as the arms and hands. Make sure the ladies' hands are done first to allow room for pockets and other decorations.

7. With the foam brushes and leather dyes, color each dress the way you want. Take your time. This is your chance to go crazy with color. Hasten the drying process with the hair dryer, if you wish.

8. Using the foam brush and buckskin dye, coat the gourd from the bottom of the dresses on down, covering the bottom of the gourd. Do the same to the top portion, including the stem. Dry everything thoroughly with the hair dryer.

9. Use black leather dye and the small artist paintbrush to color in all the heads, arms, hands, and legs. Dry them thoroughly, too.

10. Apply clear satin lacquer spray finish to the entire gourd. Let the gourd dry thoroughly between coats.

Carving the Details

11. The last step is to create the tiny carvings that will cut through the lacquer and the dye to reveal the light-colored inner skin of the gourd. Using the cylinder square cut bur, practice carving tiny shapes on the pieces of gourd scrap. Then carve on the gourd itself, using the photo to give you some ideas. Carve little squares, circles, and short straight lines to embellish the ladies with earrings, bracelets, and designs on their dresses.

12. Use the round ball bur to carve buttons on the pockets of the dresses. Now that you've made a gourd celebrating women of the world, how about another one with male figures to celebrate women and men standing together?

117

Gourd with Clay Overlay Decoration

Nature provides the three basic art materials for this awesome bowl: gourd, clay, and reed. The unusual element is the self-hardening Mexican clay, which comes in a moist form that's ready to use, and doesn't require a kiln or oven to harden.

Materials

Gourd with a small top, cleaned

Mexican self-hardening red clay (can be purchased at a craft store)

#2 round basket reed, 24 inches (61 cm) long

Leather dyes: light brown, black, buckskin

Black waxed linen thread

Tools and Supplies

Small precision jigsaw or handsaw (see page 15)

Pyrography tool with straight-line burning tip

Hair dryer

Pencil

1-inch (2.5 cm) foam brushes

Small artist paintbrush, size 4 flat shader

Butter knife

Cutting and Coloring the Gourd

1. With the angle-cut technique described on page 17, cut the tip off the gourd, leaving a small opening.

2. Approximately one quarter of the way down from the top of the gourd rim, use the pencil to draw a line composed of four arcs. See the photo for guidance. The connecting arcs will form four corners.

3. Make another line about ½ inch (1.3 cm) down from the first line. It's not necessary to measure this line exactly. Uneven lines give this project an artistic look.

4. Burn in these lines with the straight-line burning tip.

5. Use the foam brush to dye the top section of the gourd light brown. Dry with the hair dryer.

6. Apply black leather dye between the two burned lines with the paintbrush. Hasten drying time by using the hair dryer.

7. Dye the round reed with the black dye and let it dry.

8. Dye the remaining gourd with buckskin dye, using the foam brush. Dry with the hair dryer. You won't spray this gourd as you have the others, because the clay embellishments won't stick if you do.

Making the Clay Embellishments

9. Follow the manufacturer's recommendations on the box of clay. Roll out a small slab of clay. Use the butter knife to cut two wide rectangles, about ½ inch (1.3 cm) wide by 1 inch (2.5 cm) long. These can vary a bit in size. Also cut a long, thin rectangle, about ¼ inch wide (6 mm) by 1½ inches (3.8 cm) long.

10. Cut the round basket reed into a length of 1½ inches (3.8 cm). Lay the reed onto the gourd and hold it in place while you adhere the two wider clay rectangles to the center of the reed. Leave a small space between the pieces of clay.

11. Center the long, thin rectangle of clay at a 90° angle between the other two pieces, so that it over-hangs them equally at each end.

12. Use the pointed end of the pencil to make the round indentions in the clay. (See the photo.)

13. Repeat steps 9 through 12 and place clay embellishments at random intervals around the entire gourd. Increase adhesion of the clay by making cross-hatch scratches with the butter knife on the clay at the point of connection.

14. As a final decorative flourish, knot short pieces of waxed linen thread onto the mounted basket reeds where they meet the clay rectangles. Using Mexican clay, you can embellish your gourds with handmade handles, buttons and beads, add textures to a mask, and make feet for any uneven gourd bottoms.

Dyan Mai Peterson, *Bean Pot,* 1995, leather dyes, Mexican clay handles, artificial sinew rim. Photo by Tim Barnwell

Templates

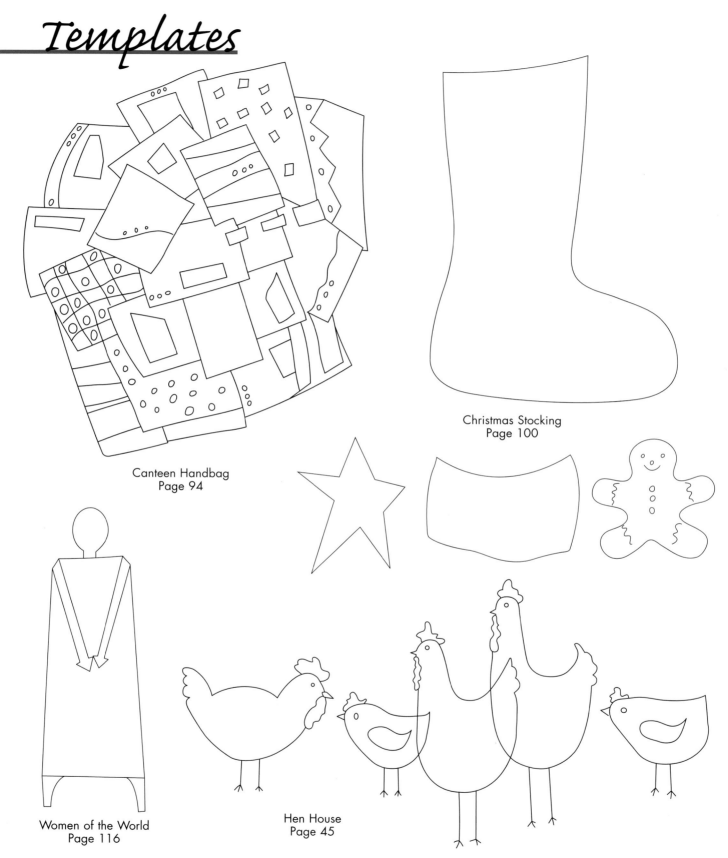

Canteen Handbag
Page 94

Christmas Stocking
Page 100

Women of the World
Page 116

Hen House
Page 45

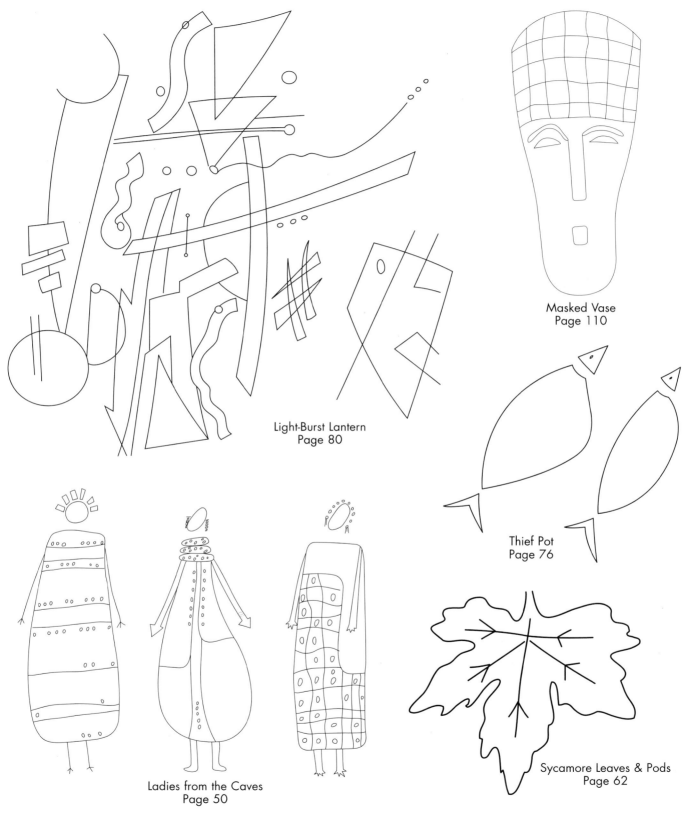

Masked Vase
Page 110

Light-Burst Lantern
Page 80

Thief Pot
Page 76

Ladies from the Caves
Page 50

Sycamore Leaves & Pods
Page 62

Dotted Horse Utensil Holder
Page 78

Beaded Mask
Page 32

Vacation Clock
Page 40

Carved Flowers
Page 56

Harvest Basket
Page 97

Debra Muhl, *Untitled #908*, 1997, gourd, Maine sweet grass, waxed Irish linen, glass beads, Photo by David Coulter

Virginia Saunders, *Butterfly*, 2000, teneriffe (woven with raffia) butterfly pattern with pine needle rim and decoration. Photo by Evan Bracken

Ronna Wuttke, *Elephant*, 2001, pyrography. Photo by Evan Bracken

David E. Blackwell, *Untitled*, 2000, small kettle gourd with long leaf pine needles. Photo by Evan Bracken

Dyan Mai Peterson, *The Actor*, 2001, paper, cloth, leather dyes, pyrography, beads. Photo by Evan Bracken

Gale Trujillo, *Replica of late 19th Century Jack-O-Lanterns*, 2000, tea-stained paper, wire. Photo by Evan Bracken

Jana White, *Three Expressions*, 2000, horsehair, acrylic paint, caulking, gourds, gourd pieces, waxed linen thread. Photo by Evan Bracken

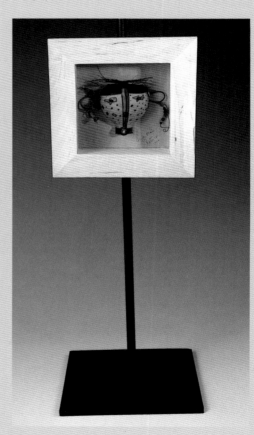

Dyan Mai Peterson, *Minature Mask*, 2001, leather dyes, felt-tip pens, grapevine, beads. Photo by Evan Bracken

Debra Toth, *Singing Gourd Men II*, 2001, carving, leather dyes, gourd vines in a shadow box frame. Photo by Diane Davis

Dyan Mai Peterson, *Taking Your Boxers for a Walk*, 2000, carved, pyrography, leather dyes, rim treatment of reed and waxed linen thread. Photo by Tm Barnwell

Debra Toth, (left to right) *Jam Session, Crisp and to the Point,* and *Are There Angels Now?*, 2000, carved gourds, leather dyes. Photo by Diane Davis

Dyan Mai Peterson, *One Red Pot*, 2000, carved, pyrography, leather dye, reed, waxed linen thread. Photo by Evan Bracken

Chris Beussink, *Air Born*, dye, pyrography, 2000. Photo by Randy Beussink

Dyan Mai Peterson, *Three Harvest Baskets*, 1996, leather dyes, (on left: rim of reed). Photo by Tim Barnwell

Judy Mofield Mallow, *Untitled*, 1999, gourd, pine needle coiling. Photo by McKenzie Photography

Acknowledgments

I was blessed with a wonderful team of talented people who helped me grow my ideas about gourd art and harvest them into this book. My heartfelt thanks go to each of them:

Editor Marcianne Miller, who in the process of becoming my dear friend was the best editor an author could have

Becky Orr, who gave generously of her help, support, and friendship during the long hours of typing the manuscript

Senior Editor Deborah Morgenthal, who started the gourds rolling by inviting me to fulfill a lifelong dream by writing this book

Photographers Evan Bracken and Tim Barnwell, whose magical ways with light captured on film the essence of the all the book's gourd art; and David Wuttke, who traveled many miles to bring back unique images of gourds in the field

Photo stylist Chris Bryant, who presented my work with the simplicity I'd hoped for; and Art Director Kathleen J. Holmes, who put all the words and images together on the final pages with elegant style and good humor

My friends and colleagues whose art appears in the gallery photos throughout the book.

The gourd farmers who generously allowed us to use photos of their gourds and gourd farms: Harry Hurley of Fuquay-Barina, NC; Jim Story of Pendleton, IN; Terry Holdsclaw, of Terrell, NC; Lena Braswell of The Gourd Farm, Wrens, GA; and Ellen Dalton of Pumpkin Hollow Gourd Farm, Piggott, AK

Members of the North Carolina Gourd Patch Society, who created the beautiful Christmas ornaments for the Festival of Trees 2001, sponsored by the Mountain Area Hospice Foundation, Asheville, NC; and especially Will Ferrell, who donated more than 150 cleaned ornamental gourds.

The American Gourd Society is dedicated to bringing information, fellowship, and support to gourd lovers all over the world. I encourage you to begin your gourd journey, or enhance it if you've already started, by contacting them.

American Gourd Society Inc.
317 Maple Ct.
Kokomo IN 46902-3633
www.americangourdsociety.org

Contributing Designers

Chris Beussink is a gourd artist who loves to embellish gourds with treasures, such as vines, ropes, wire, odds and ends, recycled materials, and anything else she can get her hands on. She shares her St. Louis, MO home and gourd-filled backyard with husband, Randy and son, Jack. cbeussink@hotmail.com.

David E. Blackwell claims he "lives firmly in the 19th century", expressing his love of simple, hand-done things with his gourd art technique of hand-chipped carving. He also does gourd pyrography in Celtic key pattern designs. He lives in Stanley, NC. (704) 258-8521

Steven Forbes-deSoule is a well-known ceramist who specializes in raku with fantastic metallic glazes. His work is exhibited in select galleries throughout the Southeast. He and his wife, Lynn Powell-Forbes, live in an intentional community in the Blue Ridge Mountains near Asheville, NC. www.stevenforbesdesoule.com.

Judy Mofield Mallow is an internationally known fiber artist, fifth generation basketmaker, and master gourd artist. She teaches in her studio in Whispering Pines, NC. http://primpines.com

Debora Muhl is a self-taught basket artist from Spinnerstown, PA. She specializes in the coiling technique, using Maine sweet grass with waxed linen and artificial sinew. She often coils around gourds to make free-form sculptures. www.deborahmuhl.com

Dyan Mai Peterson is an internationally known gourd artist and basketmaker. She lives in Asheville, NC, with her husband, furniture maker Gary Peterson. dyanmai.peterson@verizon.net and www.thedecoratedgourd.com

Virginia Saunders is a basketmaker and passionate gourd artist who specializes in southwestern motifs. She is an avid gourd gardener in Barnardsville, NC. virgbeg@main.nc.us

Debra Toth first discovered gourds while gardening at her home in Midland, NC. She soon began exploring design possibilities and now exhibits her work nationally. debra@synernet.com

Gale Trujillo concentrates her creative energies in decorating small gourds, which are featured in specialty shops and galleries on Long Island. She lives in East Moriches, NY, with her husband, Dwight Trujillo, a silversmith. (631) 286-1660

Jana White is an artist/designer who began her artistic career with gourds and now works in many other media. She lives and works in Asheville, NC. (828) 253-0668

Ronna Wuttke is a national award-winning gourd artist, especially recognized for her pyrography skills. Her Turtle Feathers studio is in Ridgeland, SC. http://surf.to/gourds. (843) 987-6643

Index

While trees lose their leaves, curing gourds grow into their dried beauty. Photo by Ellen Dalton

A wagonload of gourds will soon head out of the gourd farm for a local farmer's market. Will one of the gourds be your next piece of gourd art? Photo by David Wuttke